T0195680

"I HAVE KEPT THE FAITH"

"I have fought a good fight,
I have finished my course,
I have kept the faith!"

Albert & Aimee Anderson

authorHOUSE®

AuthorHouse™
1663 Liberty Drive
Bloomington, IN 47403
www.authorhouse.com
Phone: 833-262-8899

Published by AuthorHouse 10/07/2021

ISBN: 978-1-6655-3800-8 (sc)
ISBN: 978-1-6655-3801-5 (hc)
ISBN: 978-1-6655-3815-2 (e)

Library of Congress Control Number: 2021918850

Scripture taken from The Holy Bible, King James Version. Public Domain

"I HAVE KEPT THE FAITH"

is

In memory of my dear husband:

ALBERT EMMANUEL ANDERSON

(2013)

(A quote from Albert's BITTER OR BETTER sermon).

"No one can control all the circumstances and events that come to us day by day. Oftentimes things happen which we have no control over. However, each one of us CAN control our REACTION to what transpires in our lives. We can make a conscious choice whether we will allow the events of our lives to make us BITTER or BETTER. We can become BITTER as acid---mean, sour, miserable to be with or near---or we can use (with God's grace and help) the happenings of our lives to make us more loving, kind, considerate of others---more like Jesus!"

Bless the Lord, O my soul: and all that is within me, bless his holy name.

Bless the Lord, O my soul, and forget not all his benefits:

Who forgiveth all thine iniquities; who healeth all thy diseases; (Psalm 103:1-3)

If we say that we have no sin, we deceive ourselves, and the truth is not in us.

If we confess our sins, he is faithful and just to forgive us our sins, and to cleanse us from all unrighteousness. (I John 1:8-9)

"I have fought a good fight, I have finished my course,
"I have kept the faith:"

****

FIRST SECTION:

Some of many, Gospel messages / sermons,
that were written and preached by: Albert E. Anderson.

SECOND SECTION:

A brief review of: four, 'Personal Life' books, written by Aimee
Filan Anderson and Albert E. Anderson.

A brief review of: four, 'True' Historical Expose' books, written
by: Albert and Aimee Anderson.

A brief review of our (personal) family's, 'True-Life' movie,
written and produced by: Shawn Justice and Aimee Filan Anderson.

Acknowledgments

I express my profound appreciation and thanks to my daughter, Deborah Anderson Chase, for her loving and gracious, "FOREWORD."

I express my profound appreciation and thanks to my son, Jonathan Anderson, for his great help in editing his Dad's Gospel sermons/messages."

I wish to express my profound appreciation and thanks to Larissa Chase Budreau, my granddaughter (Deborah and Larry's daughter) for designing the beautiful COVER of this book.

Most of all with great thankfulness I acknowledge the profound and eternal truths from the Inspired Word of God, the Holy Bible. The main source of scripture quotations used in this book is from the King James Version of the Bible.

Dedication

We dedicate this book,

To: our wonderful Heavenly Father who has always been with us, and is so faithful and gracious to us.

To: all of our precious children, grandchildren, and great grandchildren.

To: Whosoever will, may you feel the sweet presence of the Holy Spirit, our Wonderful Heavenly Comforter, minister to you as you read the Gospel Messages.

Special Thanks

To our wonderful Heavenly Father: for His faithful, loving, patient, and persistent dealings in our lives to make us more like Him. In addition, we give our Lord, a special great big heart-felt, thanks for the Holy Word of God, and the eternal and everlasting principles of faith, hope, and love contained therein that daily inspire and guide us in paths of righteousness.

To my parents: Olaus and Minnie Filan (Aimee's deceased father and mother) and Albert and Hazel Anderson (Albert's deceased father and mother). We are grateful to the Lord for the godly influence our parents exerted on us. We consider ourselves blessed and enriched. We are thankful for our heritage; knowing our parents are "at home" with the Lord.

To my (11) precious beautiful children: daughter Deborah and her husband Larry, daughter Rebecca and her husband David, daughter Mary and her husband Joseph, daughter Eunice and her husband Mike, son Mark and his wife Vonda, and son Jonathan, who continue to give their love and encouragement to me. My heart is full to overflowing with love for *all* of our precious children, grandchildren, and great grandchildren.

To my (34) thirty-four precious beautiful grandchildren: Larissa and her husband David, Matthew and his wife Jasmine, Charity and her husband Tyler, Starr and her husband Sean, Benjamin and his wife Katie, Tyler and his wife Sarah, John and his wife Erin, Jordan, Joseph, Jameson and his wife Addie, Kendrin and her husband Ian, Emil and his wife Alicia, Kristina and her husband Steve, Breanna

And her husband Zach, Ali, Zach, Jordan, Zach, and Alexa who also continue to give us so much joy and love. (William, and his wife, Asma, and Clinton, are new to our family, but, now I claim them as three more "gifts from God, making a new total of 34 grandchildren, including the ones who have married into our family.)

To my (27) twenty-seven precious beautiful great grandchildren: Hailey, Ethan, Jubilee, Jesse, Annibelle, Tristan, Heston, and his wife Keziah, AimeLyn, Samantha, Tucker, Liliana, Brooklyn, Hudson, Brayden, Amelia, Lucas, Hamilton, Odelia, Merik, Atlen, Raelle, Rena Nora, Sophia, Nash, and Baily. I am so thrilled and delighted to receive these beautiful gifts of love straight from Heaven. God daily reminds me that *He is still with me/us.* All, of my children, grandchildren, and great grandchildren continue to thrill and delight me with their love and beauty. I daily name them all off to God in prayer, asking our Wonderful Father in Heaven to watch over each of my children, asking Him to please keep all of them safe in His Care and Love. My heart is big enough to love and cherish as many children, grandchildren, and greatgrandchildren that God gives to me. I love it! "Thank you, Lord God of Heaven and Earth, for my precious family."

Finally, I wish to express my deep heart-felt thanks and gratefulness to and for my dear precious (deceased, March 9, 2013) husband, Albert: for the constant inspiration, encouragement, earnest prayers, loyalty, faithfulness, and devoted love we received from each other as husband and wife for (almost 59 awesome years) fifty-eight years and eleven months to the day. I have always been very grateful and thankful to the Lord for giving me this earthly treasure, 'A Godly Husband'. And, I wish to thank Albert (in Heaven) for his wonderful Gospel messages, he daily lived and preached, as well as, his beautiful and very sweet **LOVE LETTERS**, and, for, **OUR AWESOME LOVE,** that we shared through the many years.

Foreword

By: daughter: Deborah Dawn Anderson Chase

As the oldest of the six children of Albert E and Aimee D Anderson, I have always seemed to carry the torch for our family legacy. I have "great" and "awesome" memories of the many sermons my dad preached throughout his years of ministry in the pulpit, as well as the "many" sermons that were preached to us kids before and during our times of discipline after doing something we were told not to do! Both were invaluable in my upbringing; and I will always be grateful for that.

I know beyond a shadow of a doubt that this book will be an invaluable tool for the "new" Christian just beginning his journey, the "seasoned" Christian wanting a deeper walk with the Lord, or the person that is simply "searching" for something that is missing in their lives! Jesus wants to be sought after by all humanity; and it is only after finding "HIM" the giver of life, that true happiness lies. May you be as blessed reading this book as I was living it day in and day out!

"Hast thou not known? hast thou not heard, that the everlasting God, LORD, the Creator of the ends of the earth, fainteth not, neither is weary? there is no searching of his understanding.

He giveth power to the faint; and to them that have no might he increaseth strength.

Even the youths shall faint and be weary, and the young men shall utterly fall:

But they that wait upon the Lord shall renew their strength; they shall mount up with wings as eagles; they shall run, and not be weary; and they shall walk, and not faint." Isaiah 40:28–31

First Section

Gospel messages / sermons, that were written and preached by: Albert E. Anderson.

Many of Albert's sermons, he wrote or typed in 'outline form' and while preaching he would adlib as he was inspired by the Holy Spirit. The messages / sermons, contained in this book, are as he typed them years ago, only with a very few minor typo corrections. He continued preaching and teaching the same Word of God, that he had always preached, even after he was excommunicated from two different Church Denominations for Whistle Blowing. He refused to be silenced; they could not silence him, he continued on preaching and proclaiming the Gospel of our Lord Jesus Christ!

RADIO MESSAGE

Walla Walla, Washington
8/23/53
&
RADIO MESSAGE
Monette, MO
10/11/55

SALVATION

Salvation or Religion? Which?

"Neither is their salvation in any other: for there is none other name under heaven given among men, whereby we must be saved." Acts 4:12.

How often the Bible speaks of "salvation," of being saved, of deliverance from sin's bondage, and of redemption through Jesus Christ; the reward thereby being "eternal life." Yet upon hearing the majority of people speaking on spiritual matters, they use an entirely different word to express themselves: "religion".

Let us gain an understanding of these two terms: "<u>Salvation</u>" "The redemption of man from the bondage of sin and liability to eternal death, and the conferring on him of everlasting happiness."

"Religion" the cultural act or form by which man indicates their recognition of the existence of a God or gods having power over their destiny or simply a system of faith and worship."

However, the Bible definition makes a somewhat different application of the term "religion;" James I:27 says: "pure religion

1

and undefiled before God and the Father is this, to visit the fatherless and widows in their affliction, and to keep himself unspotted from the world." The latter part especially referring to the inner soul of man.

It is true that God desires our "religion" to be manifested in outward conduct; however, such is impossible until sin has been taken from our lives and life imparted to us through Jesus Christ.

Titus 3:4-7 "But after that the kindness and love of God our Saviour toward man appeared, Not by works of righteousness which we have done, but according to his mercy he saved us, by the washing of regeneration, and renewing of the Holy Ghost; Which he shed on us abundantly through Jesus Christ our Saviour; That being justified by his grace, we should be made heirs according to the hope of eternal life."

Now, after being saved from sin, we have the responsibility of "manifesting" our good works or to term it otherwise – our "religion," or Christianity. Notice the words of our text again – "none other name" – only the name, the person of the Lord Jesus Christ. Oh, doesn't that make it simple? We need not worry about the correct church affiliation, whether we possess and believe the right creed or articles of faith, but simply, do we know the Lord Jesus Christ as our personal Saviour?

Many times, through the Scriptures, God has clearly revealed the one way of life to be found in the Lord Jesus Christ.

Religion consists in attention to rites, forms, ceremonies, precepts, laws and commandments; whereas salvation consists in the imparting of a new life by the receiving of a person. (John 1:12) Religion is what man does for God: Salvation is what God does for man.

Religion depends on our behaving: Salvation depends on our believing. (Acts 16:31).

Religion tries to bring us from the darkness to light: but Salvation "DOES" bring us from death into life. ...

"All we like sheep have gone astray; we have turned everyone to his own way; and the LORD hath laid on him the iniquity of us all." (Isaiah 53:6)

RADIO MESSAGE

Walla Walla, Washington
8/30/53
RADIO MESSAGE
Monette, MO
10/15/55
RADIO MESSAGE
PROSSER, WASHINGTON
3/23/58
&
PACKWOOD, WASHINGTON
3/23//63

"REDEMPTION"

"Forasmuch as you know that you were not redeemed with corruptible things, as silver and gold, from your vein conversation received by tradition from your father; "but with the precious blood of Christ, as of a lamb without blemish and without spot." (1 Peter 1:18-19)

The very word "Redemption" implies that we are by nature in a very evil state. It suggests a state of bondage, of slavery and oppression.

I.   THE PURPOSE OF OUR REDEMPTION

     a. In the words of Paul . . . "Ye are not your own; ye are bought with a price" (1 Corinthians 6:19–20)

b. Returning to the words of Peter, it can be expressed thus: "redeemed from your empty manner of life received by tradition from your fathers.

c. In the original, three words are used to denote redemption: (1) To deliver by the payment of a price; (2) to purchase out of the market; and (3) to liberate. --- But thinking of the purpose of our Redemption---it is true, redemption is to liberate a lost, sin-cursed race from the bondage of sin. However that is only part of it. The complete purpose was not only to free from sin, not only to deliver; but to purchase for the possession of another. It is of primary importance to the Lord that we not only find deliverance in Him, but that we then become the property of another even Jesus. Upon the completion of our deliverance, we no longer are a possession of the world, sin and Satan; but the prize possession of our Savior, the purchase price being his own blood.

Before being redeemed every person is simply a "child of the devil". Perhaps that sounds cruel or harsh --- but it is nonetheless the clear teaching of God's eternal Word. It will do us no good to attempt to squirm from beneath the sentence of death, by our own doing. Better it is, to face the issue, recognize our need and cry out as the publican of old --- Lord be merciful to me a sinner." Then and then alone shall we know not only deliverance from sin's bondage, but equally as wonderful the knowledge of belonging to the Lord Jesus --- His own treasure --- a purchased possession.

Immediately then, there follows the divine responsibility of obeying the voice of the Lord in daily, consistent Christian living. Or as the Apostle Paul puts it, (II Corinthians 5:15) "and that He died for all, that they which live should not henceforth live unto themselves, but unto Him which died for them, and rose again."

Having then become the recipients of His love and grace; how ungrateful for people to sidestep the teaching of the Scripture --- "Ye are not your own, ye are bought with a price."

II. THE COST OF OUR REDEMPTION --- In this same verse we read --- "We were not redeemed with corruptible things as silver and gold --- but, with the precious blood of Christ."

Have these words ever pierced your soul; has this message ever fastened itself upon you? --- the price of your redemption, was blood, the blood of God. Let no one think their eternal, never-dying soul is of little value --- far from it!! In the sight of God your soul is of priceless value --- this is proven in that God gave His greatest treasure, Jesus, to redeem your soul. Oh, let's make it personal --- so many times we quote; ("For God so loved the world...") that we lose individuality in numbers. It can become so general, that it fails to be specific. Just as well it could be said, ... God so loved John Brown, Mary Jones...

Therefore, we can say that the greatness of the cost speaks to us of the value of the thing purchased; for we estimate the value of an object by its purchase price.

But let us go a step farther. Because the purchase price is so great, any substitution on our part comprises the grossest sin. It is a most condemning sin to cast aside the blood of Jesus, the only means of redemption, in preference to our own way. The Bible says, "There is a way which seemeth right unto a man, but the end thereof are the ways of death."

And again, (Hebrews 10:28-29) --- "He that despised Moses' law died without mercy under two or three witnesses: Of how much sorer punishment, suppose ye, shall he be thought worthy, who hath trodden underfoot the Son of God, and hath counted the blood of the covenant, wherewith he was sanctified, an unholy thing, and hath done despite unto the Spirit of grace?

Make no mistake friends --- "without the shedding of blood there is no remission of sins" and without the application of that shed blood to your individual soul you cannot be redeemed. "A simple illustration will make this very clear --- (Ill. Of a soap salesman and preacher)".

Those who have experience "Redemption" through the blood of Jesus can sing with great joy: . . .

The triumphant cry of Jesus on the Cross --- "It is finished" is for you in this 20th century. Won't you simply believe the word of the Lord, trust in the finished work of Christ and allow Him to be all you need.

III. THE SCOPE OF OUR REDEMPTION:

A. "Christ hath redeemed us from the curse of the law... that we might receive the promise of the Spirit through faith." (Gal. 3:13-14)

"...That he might redeem us from all iniquity . . .." (Titus 2:14)

Waiting for the adoption, to wit, the redemption of our body." (Romans 8:23)

Bless the Lord, O my soul: and all that is within me, bless his holy name.

Blessed Lord, O my soul, and forget not all his benefits:

Who forgiveth all thine iniquities; who healeth all thy diseases;

Who redeemeth thy life from destruction; who crowneth thee with lovingkindness and tender mercies;

Who satisfieth thy mouth with good things; so that thy youth is renewed like the eagle's. (Psalm 103:1-5)

RADIO MESSAGE

Walla Walla, Washington
9/6/53
RADIO MESSAGE
Monette, MO
10/12/55

<u>WORSHIP</u>

"But the hour cometh, and now is, when the true worshippers shall worship the Father in spirit and in truth: for the Father seeketh such to worship him. God is a Spirit: And they that worship him must worship him in spirit and in truth." John 4:23-24.

The Scripture says --- "the Father seeks worshippers.". here again we see the marvelous love and grace of God. From the time man first fell this principle has obtained. First, God seeking man to free him from his sin, and now God again seeking redeemed man to worship Him.

The Father seeks worshippers: our worship satisfies His loving heart and is a joy to Him. He seeks True worshippers, but is often disappointed in His seeking. True worship is that which is in Spirit and in Truth.

In speaking to the woman at the well, Jesus spoke of a three-fold worship. First, there was the ignorant worship of the Samaritans --- "Ye worship that which ye know not." Second, the more complete or intelligent worship of the Jew --- "We worship that which we know; for salvation is of the Jews." And then the new worship which He,

8

Christ, came to introduce. "The hour is coming, and now is, when the true worshipers shall worship the father in spirit and in truth."

From the connection, it is evident that the words, "in spirit and in truth", do not mean simply sincerity. The Samaritans were sincere – even as many people today. The Jews had the books of Moses and many knew God. Yet Jesus said that the hour is coming and now is "– in other words, it is only in and through Christ that anyone can please the father in worshiping "in spirit and in truth".

It seems we still find today these three classes of worshipers. Are you in the first group – etc.

The first and most important brought forth by the Lord here is that there must be HARMONY between God and his worshipers. And it is right at this point that many people stumble and utterly fail God. Multitudes, not only in heathen lands, but even in so-called "Christian America", seek to bring a FORM of worship unto the Lord. And in so doing bypass the very one who could bring them into true worship to God. Observe thousands as they make their way to houses of worship every Lord's day. There are many in our own city of Walla Walla. See them as they go! For six days, their thoughts have not been of God – except perhaps as many have taken His name in vain. For six days and not improbably a good portion of the Lord's day they have lived for self alone, indulged in sin. Yet on the designated Lord's Day they seek to pay their respects to a God they've openly denied and rejected all week. And the tragedy of it all is, that they are so foolish as to believe that God is pleased with their faithful attendance at the house of worship. Live as they please and as the devil dictates, just so long as they are found piously seated in the same house of worship on Sunday morning.

Oh, do not be deluded by the lies of Satan. Heed not the subtle whisperings of the arc-enemy of your eternal soul; who would have you believe all is well because you merely attend the house of God and follow through a dead form of worship; while in reality you know nothing of the saving power of the Lord Jesus Christ. Rather seek Him who alone can bring you into right relationship to God so that you can truly worship God in "spirit and in truth".

God hates any form of worship which is separated from true righteousness and godly living. God's people, Israel, had fallen into the same deception and in the book of Amos 5:21-24, we read --- "I hate, I despise your feast days, and I will not smell in your solemn assemblies. Though ye offer me burnt-offerings and your meat-offerings, I will not accept them: neither will I regard the peace offerings of your fat beasts. Take thou away from me the noise of thy songs; for I will not hear the melody of thy viols. But let judgment run down as waters, and righteousness as a mighty stream."

And again, the Bible says in Proverbs. 21:27 "The sacrifice of the wicked is abomination: how much more, when he bringeth it with a wicked mind?" Once more in Proverbs, 28:9 "He that turneth away his ear from hearing the law, even his prayer shall be abomination."

And from the book of Jeremiah 7:22-23. "For I spake not unto your fathers, nor commanded them in the day that I brought them out of the land of Egypt, concerning burnt offerings or sacrifices: But this thing commanded I them, saying, Obey my voice, and I will be your God, and ye shall be my people: and walk ye in all the ways that I have commanded you:". . .

So, it is clearly evident that the first prime essential in worshipping God is to be brought into right relationship to God through Jesus Christ. And not only to have been brought into right relationship with God; but to live in harmony with God daily. Then alone is it possible to worship God, "in spirit and in truth". Moreover, as you live in touch with God daily, you will find worship in spirit and truth is possible anywhere, anytime; for as God is Spirit, not bound by space or time, so His worship is not confined by place or form, but spiritual as God Himself is spiritual.

RADIO MESSAGE

Walla Walla, Washington
9/13/53

RAPTURE

THE RAPTURE OF THE CHURCH

In reading the Scriptures one cannot help but see revealed one of the most glorious doctrines contained in all the Holy Scriptures; namely, the rapture of the church the catching up of all true believers in Christ to meet the Lord in the air. This event is simply and clearly predicted in a number of passages in the New Testament. To the child of God, it is a time for which we look with longing anticipation.

However, in spite of it being clearly evident in the Word of God, there are those who deny that such an event will ever take place. But denial of what God said will definitely take place does not change the Word of the Lord.

As an example of the places it is mentioned in the scripture: the apostle Paul says in first I Thessalonians 4:16, 17, "For the Lord himself shall descend from heaven with a shout, with the voice of the archangel, and with the Trump of God: and the dead in Christ shall rise first: Then we which are alive and remain shall be caught up together with them in the clouds, to meet the Lord in the air: and so shall we ever be with the Lord."

We need not be ignorant concerning this subject because it is fully and clearly revealed in many passages of the New Testament. The fact and manner of the rapture are clearly revealed in the following scriptures: Jesus said, "Watch ye therefore, and pray always, that ye may be accounted worthy to escape all these things that shall come to pass, and to stand before the Son of man." Jesus said in Luke 21:36, "And if I go and prepare a place for you, I will come again, and receive you unto myself; that where I am, there ye may be also" and John 14:3. I Corinthians:15:51, "Behold, I shew you a mystery, We shall not all sleep, but we shall all be changed, In a moment, in the twinkling of an eye, at the last trump: for the trumpet shall sound, and the dead shall be raised incorruptible, and we shall all be changed.", . . .

What does the rapture mean? In the Greek, we have two words referring to the rapture.

1. Parousia – meaning, personal coming or appearance. At the rapture, Christ appears personally in the air to meet the Saints.
2. Then, Phaneros, which means to shine, be apparent, manifest or be seen.

THE PURPOSE OF THE RAPTURE:

The purpose of the rapture is to resurrect the just from the dead and take all the saints out of the world before the tribulation comes, in order that they may have fulfilled in them the purpose for which God has saved them.

THE QUALIFICATIONS FOR THE RAPTURE:

The qualifications for partakers in the rapture also revealed in the Scripture, contrary to some. The one and only necessary requirement for men, whether they are dead or alive, is to be "in Christ". Briefly this qualification is stated in a nine-fold way in scripture.

1. Be "Christ's",
2. "in Christ",

3. Be "blessed and Holy",
4. "Have done good",
5. Be in "the way, the truth and the life",
6. Be "worthy",
7. "Be in the church or body of Christ",
8. Purify "himself, even as He is pure",
9. Be without "spot or wrinkle … and without blemish".

If one has met these scriptural qualifications, what more could he do? This implies that a person going up in the rapture is walking in "the light, as he is in the light". Being "in Christ" (II Corinthians 5:17b-18a) means that one is a new creature: old things are passed away; behold, all things are become new. And all things are of God, who hath reconciled us to himself by Jesus Christ." To belong to Christ simply means that they have "crucified the flesh with the affections and lusts". This means they are good, holy, blessed, and free from the sin business. What better qualifications for the rapture could God require. Now these qualifications have been taken directly from those passages and definitely deal with the rapture. If there were other qualifications or those that were more definite and important, wouldn't they have been stated in the passages on the rapture in the place of these that have been given? We conclude then that it is not receiving other experiences, whatever they may be, or however scriptural they may be, that qualifies one to go up in the rapture, but it is the maintenance of a holy walk "in Christ" at the time of the rapture or at the time of death as the case may be.

THE TIME OF THE RAPTURE:

As to the time of the rapture, we don't have that revealed to us in the scripture. Hence, the importance of being ready at any time.

THIS IS A PRACTICAL DOCTRINE:

The rapture is a real incentive to holiness: profitable and exhorting to watchfulness and faithfulness, patience, death to self, endurance, holy conversation and godliness, etc. The rapture to the saints will be the beginning of eternal and ever increasing joy and glory.

RADIO MESSAGE

Walla Walla, Washington
9/20/53
RADIO MESSAGE
PROSSER, WASHINGTON
8/17/58

"THE WORD OF GOD"

"But continue thou in the things which thou hast learned and hast been assured of, knowing of whom thou hast learned them; And that from a child thou hast known the holy scriptures, which are able to make thee wise unto salvation through faith which is in Christ Jesus. All scripture is given by inspiration of God, and is profitable for doctrine, for reproof, for correction, for instruction in righteousness: That the man of God may be perfect, throughly furnished unto all good works." 2 Timothy 3:14-17. . .

With such a wonderful book at our disposal, one would think that every person living today would ever study and live according to the Bible. However, one is sadly disappointed when observing multitudes who scarcely ever turn its pages, let alone study it. One of the reasons many people do not read and study the Bible is because they say: "It is too difficult to understand". It is almost a universal idea the Bible is hard to understand and must be changed to be understood; and that it is full of mysteries, secrets, and hidden meanings veiled in spiritual language which only a few special men of God can understand. Some believe that the Bible has many different meanings; that one man's interpretation is as good as another; and that one can prove anything from the Bible. How far from true are such ideas.

In all actuality, the Bible is the most-simple book to understand. This statement may sound hard to believe, but before you condemn such a statement; let me give you some reasons for saying the Bible is the most-simple book to understand. It is easy to understand because it is a "Revelation". Now what is a revelation: A revelation is an uncovering or unveiling so that all can see alike what was previously covered or hidden. The only excuse any man would have for not seeing something that was uncovered for him to see is his willful refusal to look. Anything that is revealed is clear, or the purpose of the revelation has failed.

Second, it is easy to understand because of its "Repeated Truths". Over and over the Bible repeats truth so that "in the mouth of two or three witnesses shall every word be established". Any doctrine that is not plainly stated in Scripture is best left alone. If God is silent on some question, then man has no right to say anything about it as taught in the Bible. Anything that is not taught in the Bible should not be taught or believed by anyone --- but leave all teachings to a strict --- "Thus saith the Lord". Personal opinion is worthless if it is not taught in the Bible. Throughout the Bible God speaks on a subject more than once. All we have to do is collect everything God has said on a subject and it will be so clear that no interpretation will be necessary. If we do this nothing will be taken from the Bible and we will not add anything that is not there. The main thing is to secure what "God" has said upon a subject and then we must "believe" it. The trouble with many people is that they reserve the right to change the Holy Scriptures as they please. The correct procedure is to make our lives conform to the Bible and not the Bible to our ideas. Anyone who presumes to know more than what God has said usurps God's place as the author of the Scriptures.

Also, the Bible is easy to understand because God is the Author of the Bible. The scripture given at the beginning of the message is a proof of this fact. If God is the author, we have every right to believe and expect it to be clear. No man can make a book more simple than God can. If God could make a book as simple to understand as man can and did not do so, then we have to conclude that He did not want man to understand His Word. If that were so then why did God give his Word to man? In that case man should discard the Bible and accuse God of injustice for judging him on something he could not understand. Since we cannot believe in such a thing we must conclude that God's Word is simple to understand and believe if we are willing to do so.

A God who could not make Himself clear, or who had to be interpreted every time He said something, would be no God at all. Almost any human being can express himself clearly enough to be understood. Furthermore, a God who could make Himself clear and chose to do otherwise in such a way as to confuse and hide from man those things He seeks to reveal to him, would not be worth hearing. A God that gave man a revelation and deliberately sought to hide it from him and then judge him for not being able to understand it, would be a tyrant instead of a God of love and justice. How foolish to even tolerate for a moment such slanderous conceptions of a loving God.

Let us believe, like sensible human beings, that God can and did speak to men in the most simple human language; that He meant exactly what He said and said exactly what He meant: that He expected men to understand it on the same basis, using the same principles of human language that they use to understand other books; that He will hold them responsible for what He says, not for what men interpret His words to say; and that He has a right to judge men in the end if they constantly make Him false in all that He says.

Furthermore, the Bible is simple because it was given by God to be understood by the simple.

God's word says in Psalm 119:130 "The entrance of thy words giveth light; it giveth understanding unto the simple."

And in the first chapter of Proverbs 1:1-4: "The proverbs of Solomon the son of David, king of Israel; To know wisdom and instruction; to perceive the words of understanding; To receive the instruction of wisdom, justice, and judgment, and equity; To give subtilty to the simple, to the young man knowledge and discretion."

Paul speaks of "The simplicity that is in Christ". Jesus thanked God that the truths of the Bible were hidden from the worldly wise who refused to believe, and stated that God has revealed them unto babes. He gives the reason truths are hidden from anyone. It is because they refuse to humble themselves to believe and conform to the Bible.

The most-simple beginners can understand the Bible one line at a time, for this is the way it was given and it is the best way to understand it. No man can get all the vastness of the Bible at once. It is the seemingly infinite scope of truth that causes some men to think the Bible is hard to understand. It is like a man arguing that he cannot understand water because he cannot drink the ocean dry at one drink. Naturally it takes time to get a simple knowledge of the whole Bible, but what we contend is this: taking a line at a time, verse at a time, or truth at a time, it cannot be hard to understand. One cannot look at any big book and get all of its contents at a glance. A man is foolish to say the Bible is hard to understand until he gets into it and gets acquainted with its contents. If a man will do this he will find the Bible truths opening up beyond his fondest dreams.

RADIO MESSAGE

Walla Walla, Washington
9/27/53

"PRAYER"

The mark of a real Christian is a desire to "grow in grace". "He cannot be satisfied with past experiences. He hungers and thirsts after righteousness, and to him, therefore, the promise is that he "shall be filled ".

Certainly, there are few Christian graces which need to grow and abound more than the growth in "PRAYER". Someone has said, "Our whole Christian life depends upon prayer." Another has said, "We are never so high as when we are on our knees." Surely no one would dispute the fact of the great necessity of prayer being an integral and vital part of every Christian's life. It is through prayer that we can come into living contact with our God.

Just what is prayer? In its simplest sense, it is simply communion or communication or yet more simply, conversation with God. In the realm of praise, it can be the offering of adoration, thanksgiving, and worship to God. Jesus said in Luke 11:2, "When ye pray, say…" In other words, simply talking to God as we would to some other person we are intimately and personally acquainted with.

Now…if prayer be such an important and foundational factor in the life of every Christian; why is it that prayer is so often lacking? Isaiah gives some important instructions concerning this: Isa. 59:1-2 "Behold, the LORD's hand is not shortened, that it cannot save;

neither his ear heavy, that it cannot hear: But your iniquities have separated between you and your God, and your sins have hid his face from you, that he will not hear." Here we see the utter necessity of having all clear between our soul and God. If we are to know sweet communion with God, we must make sure our heart does not condemn us. Paul said, (Acts 24:16) "And herein do I exercise myself, to have always a conscience void of offence toward God, and toward men." He recognized the need of a clear conscience which would not condemn him when he came to God in prayer.

Too often --- the reason we fail to have and hold communion with our "Father", is that somewhere along the line, our heart condemns us. What then must be done in order that we can freely come to God? The apostle John tells us in I John 2:16, "If any man sin, we have an advocate with the Father, Jesus Christ the righteous." Therefore, perchance there has been failure on our part, the proper and most pleasing thing to the Lord for us to do is confess it and allow the efficacy of the shed blood of Christ to cleanse from sin. If and when we do sin, we do not come to the Lord for cleansing, we do Him a great injustice, for it shows unbelief on our part which is also sin. The writer to the Hebrews tells us (Hebrews 19:22) "Having therefore, brethren, boldness to enter into the holiest by the blood of Jesus, By a new and living way, which he hath consecrated for us, through the veil, that is to say, his flesh; And having an high priest over the house of God; Let us draw near with a true heart in full assurance of faith, having our hearts sprinkled from an evil conscience, and our bodies washed with pure water." Oh, thank God, for the "new" and "living" way --- access to the very holiest presence of God.

Before the death of Christ on the cross, only the high priest, once a year could enter into the "holiest"; but now through Christ, the holiest presence of God is the rightful heritage of every child of God. Let us not fail to appropriate and attain to our position in the Lord Jesus Christ.

Having brought to you a bit of the importance of prayer, what prayer is, the importance of being right with God in order to have true fellowship with God and our rightful heritage of entering into

God's presence; let us consider for a few moments the reasons for prayer. Just WHY PRAY?

We have already given one very important reason and that is that we may talk to God, draw near unto Him. But going a bit further we notice something else most important. The Lord Jesus Himself commanded us to pray. In Luke 18:1 Jesus said, "Men ought always to pray, and not to faint." In Matthew 26:41 Jesus said, "Watch and pray, that ye enter not into temptation: the spirit indeed is willing, but the flesh is weak."

If we would please the Lord, then we must spend time in prayer for it is commanded by the Lord Himself. In John 14:21 Jesus said, "He that hath my commandments, and keepeth them, he it is that loveth me: and he that loveth me shall be loved of my Father, and I will love him, and will manifest myself to him." In this very verse there arises another very important reason for praying. That is, because of our relationship to God through Christ. And if we love the Lord, then we will automatically desire to pray. What son, who has a loving father, does not like to be with his father? What son does not like to get better acquainted with his dad? If that be true in the natural life, how much more should it be true in the spiritual realm.

Think of it: through Christ and because of Christ, we can call God "Our Father". And realizing He is our Father, our hearts should long to know Him better, to love Him more; and these things will be acquired as we come to Him in prayer.

Returning to the thought of commandment --- the apostle Paul adds a word also. He tells us in 1Thess. 5:17, "Pray without ceasing." In other words, though our physical posture might not be that of a form of prayer, yet from our heart in the midst of daily duties, we can hold fellowship and communion with God.

We are not left helpless in this matter of prayer either. Paul in Romans 8:26-27 tells us: "Likewise the Spirit also helpeth our infirmities: for we know not what we should pray for as we ought: but the Spirit itself maketh intercession for us with groanings which cannot be uttered. And he that searcheth the hearts knoweth what is the mind of the Spirit, because he maketh intercession for the saints according to the will of God."

It would do us well to discuss for a moment, "how to pray". Not only are we to "Pray without ceasing", which carries with it a time element, but also we are to pray with perseverance, with diligence and in earnestness. Jesus spoke several times dealing with the thought of being importunate in prayer. That is, not giving in to unbelief or the difficulty of the situation, but believing and praying until the request becomes living reality.

Too often people stop praying when the answer does not come immediately. Daniel prayed twenty-one days before his answer came from God…the reason being, a spiritual battle in the heavens between the angels of God and the cohorts of Satan. The answer had been sent on its way as soon as Daniel prayed, but had been delayed in route because of a spiritual conflict. Just so may it be with us many times.

Moreover, someone has said, "If it is right to pray for something, it is wrong to stop until the answer comes." For failing to persevere in prayer shows unbelief. And faith is the very requirement necessary for us to possess in order to even come to God. "But without faith it is impossible to please him; for he that cometh to God must believe that he is, and that he is a rewarder of them that diligently seek him." Hebrews 11:6.

This verse brings in our thought of diligence. Too often people go at this business of praying with little zest, feeling as though, well after all it isn't of much importance. But upon our diligence in prayer hangs the outcome of the spiritual battle which we are waging. . .

We must be earnest and fervent in our praying. James 5:16b tells us: "The effectual fervent prayer of a righteous man availeth much." It's not so much the amount of time we may spend in prayer perhaps, or how many words we say, or even if our prayers are beautifully phrased --- but it does matter about the earnestness with which we pray.

RADIO MESSAGE

Walla Walla, Washington
10/4/53
RADIO MESSAGE
PROSSER, WASHINGTON
1/4/59
&
PREACHED
By: Jonathan D. Anderson
ELLENSBURG, WASHINGTON
8/11/91

<u>FAITH</u>

Faith is defined as a thing wrought in us. It is a divine principle, a blessed power that God gives and implants within. Stephen, we read, was "full of Faith". We cannot be full of an attitude, but we surely can be full of that divine light of soul that enables us to rejoice in the Lord evermore.

It is through faith that all the blessings of God are brought to us. From the initial experience of salvation to the time when we see Jesus face to face, it will all have been attained through FAITH.

Concerning ourselves primarily, however with God's present dealings with us, there are a number of blessings received by faith which are worthy of consideration. Paul tells us in Romans 5:1-2, "Therefore being justified by faith, we have peace with God through our Lord Jesus Christ: By whom also we have access by faith into this grace wherein we stand, and rejoice in hope of the glory of God." And in Galatians 2:16, "Knowing that a man is not justified by the works of the law, but by the faith of Jesus Christ, even we have believed in Jesus Christ, that we might be justified by the faith of Christ, and not by the works of the law: for by the works of the law shall no flesh be justified." So, our being justified and made right with God through Christ is alone through faith. And even here God helps our infirmities, for he says in Ephesians 2:8-9, that "faith is the gift of God".

Speaking of SALVATION as a whole it is again by faith that we are brought to and made right with God. The Bible tells us in John 1:12, "But as many as received him, to them gave he power to become the sons of God, even to them that believe on his name:".

And again, in the most known verse of the Bible, (John 3.16), "For God so loved the world, that he gave his only begotten Son, that whosoever believeth in him should not perish, but have everlasting life." The last verse, verse 36, in this same chapter states the same requirement --- Faith! "He that believeth on the Son hath everlasting life: and he that believeth not the Son shall not see life; but the wrath of God abideth on him."

It is through Faith that peace of heart and soul is brought to us as already mentioned in Romans 5. Faith brings joy as Peter tells us: (I Peter 1:8) "Whom having not seen, ye love; in whom, though now ye see him not, yet believing, ye rejoice with joy unspeakable and full of glory:".

FAITH is the shield of the Christian giving him power over the enemy: (I Thessalonians 5:8) "But let us, who are of the day, be sober, putting on the breastplate of faith and love". And from the book of Ephesians: (Ephesians 6:16) "Above all, taking the shield of faith, wherewith ye shall be able to quench all the fiery darts of the wicked".

Seeing then the utter necessity of Faith, its extreme importance in living a victorious Christian life; we can be sure that Satan will viciously attack us on this very point. If the adversary of our souls can cause us to depart from our Faith in God, his purpose is accomplished. For it is only by faith that we are brought into living fellowship with God. Cut the life-line and we are once more adrift; completely at the mercy of the devil.

The Bible gives some very clear examples of the results of losing or forfeiting our FAITH in God. Paul in writing to Timothy warns of the danger in losing faith --- and of its terrible consequences. "Now the end of the commandment is charity out of a pure heart, and of a good conscience, and of faith unfeigned: From which some having swerved have turned aside unto vain jangling; Desiring to be teachers of the law; understanding neither what they say, nor whereof they affirm." 1Timothy 1:5-7.

"Holding faith, and a good conscience; which some having put away concerning faith have made shipwreck: of whom is Hymenaeus and Alexander; whom I have delivered unto Satan, that they may learn not to blaspheme." I Timothy 1:19.

"Now the Spirit speaketh expressly, that in the latter times some shall depart from the faith, giving head to seducing spirits, and doctrines of devils; Speaking lies in hypocrisy; having their Conscience seared with a hot iron;" I Timothy 4:1-2.

"For the love of money is the root of all evil: which while some coveted after, they erred from the faith, and pierced themselves through with many sorrows. But thou, O, man of God, flee these things; and follow after righteousness, godliness, faith, love, patience, meekness. Fight the good fight of faith, lay hold on eternal life, whereunto thou art also called, and hast professed a good profession before many witnesses." I Timothy 6:10-12.

RADIO MESSAGE

Walla Walla, Washington
10/11/53

"FRUIT-BEARING"

The barren fig tree--Matthew 21:18-19.

This incident is, from first to last, an acted parable. What then, was the lesson which on this occasion he desired to teach? Was it simply the shame and guilt of every responsible creature of God's hand, moral unfruitfulness? Did he cause the tree to wither because it was a symbol of nations and of nations who do nothing for His glory and nothing for their fellows? That he does punish such unfruitfulness is certain; but this is not the lesson he would teach us here. The time of figs was not yet. Why then did he curse it and cause it to die?

The tree was a symbol of that which, in man, is worse sin than merely a fruitless life. It had leaves, you will observe, though it had no fruit. That was the distinction of this particular tree among its fellows ranged along the road with their bare, leafless unpromising branches. They held out hopes of nothing beyond what met the eye. This tree, with its abundant leaves, gave promise of fruit that might be well-nigh ripe and thus was a symbol of moral or of religious pretentiousness. Not simply as unfruitful, but because, being unfruitful, it was covered with leaves, it was a fitting symbol of that want of correspondence between profession and practice --- between claims and reality --- between the surface appearances of life and its real direction and purpose --- which our Lord condemned so often and so sternly in the men of His time.

I.   The fig tree represented first, no doubt, The Actual State of The Jewish People. The heathen nations, judged from a Divine point of view, were barren enough. Israel was barren also, but then Israel was also pretentious and false. Israel was covered with leaves. The letter of the law --- the memories, the sepulchers of the prophets --- the ancient sacrifices --- the accredited teachers --- all were in high consideration. Israel was, to all appearances, profoundly religious. But the searching eye of our Lord found no fruit upon this tree beneath the leaves --- no true soul-controlling belief even in the promises of the Messiah, of which they made so much --- no true sense of their obligation and of their incapacity to please God. The tree by the roadside was a visible symbol of the moral condition of Israel as it presented itself to the eye of Christ, and there was no longer any reason for suspending the judgment which had been foretold in the Savior's parable: "No man eat fruit of thee hereafter for ever." (Confer Isaiah 5:1)

II. The parable applies with equal force to Nations or to churches in Christendom which make great pretentions and do little or nothing of real value to mankind. For a time the tree waves its leaves in the wind. It lives on, sustained by the traditional habits and reverence of age. But, at His own time, Christ passes along the highway --- passes to inquire and to judge: some unforeseen calamity, some public anxiety, some shock to general confidence, lifts the leaves of that tree and discovers its real fruitlessness.

III. This parable applies to every individual Christian today. The religious activity of the human soul may be divided, roughly, into leaves and fruit --- showy forms of religious activity and interest on the one side, and direct produce of religious conviction on the other. It is much easier to grow leaves than to grow fruit; and many a man's life veils the absence of fruit by the abundance of leaves. To take an interest in religious questions and discussions is better than to be totally indifferent to them; but mere acquaintance with, and interest in, such proves nothing as to the condition of the conscience --- the real condition of the heart --- the deepest movements of the inmost life --- the soul's state before God, and its prospects for eternity. An anxious question for all is, whether the foliage of our Christian life is the covering of fruit beneath that is ripening for heaven, or only a thing of precocious and unnatural growth which has drained away the tree's best sap before its time, and made good fruit almost impossible. No show of leaves, no fervor of language, no glow of feeling, no splendor of outward achievements for Christ's cause and kingdom, will compensate, in His sight, for the absence of the fruits of the Spirit. Let us consider for a moment the words of Jesus to His disciples, and also to us today, in the 15th chapter of John.

"I am the true vine, and my Father is the husbandman. Every branch in me that beareth not fruit he taketh away: and every branch that beareth fruit, he purgeth it, that it may bring forth more fruit. I am the vine, ye are the branches: He that abideth in me, and I in Him, the same bringeth forth much fruit: for without me ye can do nothing. If a man abide not in me, he is cast forth as a branch, and is withered; and men gather them, and cast them into the fire, and they are burned." (John 15:1-2, 5-6).

Here again are words which too often are taken much too lightly. Jesus is looking for fruit and has every right to do so, for he who professes to know Christ must of necessity bear fruit. Life denotes growth and growth signifies production. Therefore, if you say, "I have been saved, have been born again," then upon you rests the responsibility of bearing fruit. Christ is our life and if we are abiding in Him, fruit will be the natural outcome of our union with Him. But beware of profession without possession --- of beautiful and numerous leaves; but without any sign of fruit.

RADIO MESSAGE

Walla Walla, Washington
10/18/53
RADIO MESSAGE
PROSSER, WASHINGTON
8/10/58

"JESUS, THE SON OF GOD"

"The next day John seeth Jesus coming unto him, and saith, Behold the Lamb of God, which taketh away the sin of the world." John 1:29

Who is this Lamb of God; that is, who is the Lord Jesus Christ? This question was put by the Master Himself when, during a crisis in His ministry, He asked, "Whom do men say that I the Son of man am?" He listened to the statement of current opinion which stated --- "Some say that thou art John the Baptist; some, Elias; and others, Jeremias, or one of the prophets." Matthew 16:13-14. But His blessing was pronounced upon the answer which Peter had learned from God: "Thou art the Christ, the Son of the living God." Matthew 16:16b.

The apostle Peter had learned something which yet today many people do not understand or comprehend --- that Christ was not just another man, not just another prophet, not just another great spiritual leader --- but Jesus Christ was and is today, The Son of God --- in a sense which no other person in all the universe has experienced. . .

The question, "Who is Christ?" is best answered by stating and explaining the names and titles by which He is known.

29

First, the title, "Son of God" which refers to deity. As "son of man" means one born of man, so "Son of God" means one born of God. Hence this title proclaims the deity of Christ. Jesus is never called a Son of God, in the general sense in which men and angels are children of God. And let me insert right here, that man apart from the knowledge of Christ as Savior and Lord, are not "sons of God" in a spiritual sense, but only in the sense of being the creation of God. Before man sinned, he may well have been called a "son of God" in the spiritual sense, but Sin severed that relation and until it is once again joined together through Christ, man is none other than a child of the devil --- as even Jesus Himself taught.

Christ is The Son of God in the unique sense. Jesus is described as sustaining toward God a relationship not shared by any other person in the universe.

Luke, the only Gospel writer who describes the important incident in the boyhood of Jesus, tells us that at the age of twelve perhaps before and much earlier, Jesus was conscious of two things: one, a special relationship to God whom He describes as His Father; and second, a special mission on earth --- His Father's business.

And at the river Jordan Jesus heard the Father's voice confirming His inner consciousness (Mathew 3:17) and in the wilderness He successfully resisted Satan's attempt to question His Sonship, ("If thou be the Son of God..." Matthew 4:3). Certainly, if the young man, Jesus Christ, would have been only a great teacher or civic leader, as some so foolishly believe today, then Satan would most definitely not have attacked Him on this vital issue. But the evil and sinister forces of Satan knew this to be the Son of God in human form and therefore strived to thwart the plan of God with every possible effort. And it seems the arch enemy of our souls is still very busy today, seeking to turn men away from the revelation made known to Peter that Jesus, is "the Christ, the Son of the living God".

Moreover, when before the Jewish council, He might have escaped death by denying the unique Sonship and simply affirm that He was a son of God in the same sense that all men are; instead being put on oath by the high priest, He declared His consciousness of Deity, even though He knew it meant the death sentence.

Consider for a moment the Claims of Christ Himself: He put Himself side by side with the Divine activity by stating --- "My Father worketh hitherto, and I work," John 5:17b. "I came forth from the Father," John 16:28a. "My Father hath sent me, . . " John 20:21. He claimed a Divine knowledge and fellowship; He claimed to unveil the Father's being in Himself. He assumed Divine prerogatives: omnipresence, power to forgive sins; power to raise the dead, and He proclaimed Himself Judge and arbiter of man's destiny. He demanded a surrender and an allegiance that only God could rightly claim; He insisted on absolute self-surrender on the part of His followers.

Note something else: In Christ's teaching one notes a complete absence of such expressions as --- "It is my opinion", "It may be", "I think that", "We may well suppose", etc. Even the officers whom the Pharisees sent to catch Jesus in His words said --- "Never man spake like this man." John 7:46b. And after the sermon on the mount the people were forced to say --- much the same things for the Bible says: "And it came to pass, when Jesus had ended these sayings, the people were astonished at his doctrine: For he taught them as one having authority, and not as the scribes." Matthew 7:28-29.

Again, the SINLESSNESS of Christ proves his Deity. In the words and deeds of Jesus there is a complete absence of consciousness or confession of sin. He had the deepest knowledge of the evil of it, yet no shadow or stain of it fell upon His own soul. On the contrary, He, the humblest of men, issues the challenge, "Which of you convinceth me of sin?" (John 8:46a). And the inspired writings of the apostles bear out the nature of our Lord. Paul in II Cor. 5:21 states: "For he hath made him to be sin for us, who knew no sin; that we might be made the righteousness of God in him."

The apostle Peter reiterates this conclusion by saying: (I Peter 2:22) "Who did no sin, neither was guile found in his mouth." And the disciple of love, John, says: (I John 3:5) "And ye know that he was manifested to take away our sins; and in him is no sin." . . .

The world says --- seeing is believing. But Jesus said, "Believe and thou shalt see". Take away the deity of Christ and the foundation pillar is removed. Take away the deity of Christ and all provision for the breaking of sin's bondage is broken. And take away the power of the Christ of Calvary to forgive sin and make a soul right in the sight of God, and the world will return to jungle night.

RADIO MESSAGE

Walla Walla, Washington
10/25/53
RADIO MESSAGE
PROSSER, WASHINGTON
5/4/58
RADIO MESSAGE
MONETT, MISSOURI
10/13/55

ASSURANCE OF SALVATION

Is it possible to KNOW we are saved now in this life or do we have to wait until we die to find out what our eternal destiny will be? Does God's Word say we can KNOW now? Thank God, the answer to these and other similar questions on this subject is a definite and positive YES! And it is not merely a yes from some man but from the Word of God. Now --- if people do not want to BELIEVE the Word of God, then of course they cannot know whether they are saved or not; but to ANY person who is simply willing to BELIEVE what God has said in His Word, there comes the positive assurance of knowing they are saved NOW in this present life.

The Bible says in 1 John 5:13 --- "These things have I written unto you that believe on the name of the Son of God; that ye may know that ye have eternal life, and that ye may believe on the name of the Son of God."

This verse reveals several important points --- the most important being --- that the assurance of salvation and eternal life is given to those that have believed. Certainly the person who has never believed and therefore has never been born again can KNOW he is saved. Perhaps there are those listening even now who have falsely trusted in church membership, in good deeds and works, in doing their best, of being sincere and all the other false man-made ways of seeking to please God. And because you have trusted in these things, perhaps when alone or in an hour of trial you think --- "I wonder if everything is all right between my soul and God after all." In other words --- because you have not believed and therefore have not received Christ as your Savior --- you do not know if you are saved and naturally you cannot KNOW.

Let us see what kind of believing the Bible talks about. And, what are some of the evidences of being born again as a result of truly believing in the Son of God as John wrote and therefore knowing we are saved.

1. If you have been born again you will have been changed down in the depths of your being and will have been made a new creature. For the Bible says: (II Corinthians 5:17) "Therefore if any man be in Christ, he is a new creature: old things are passed away; behold, all things are become new." If you have never been changed like this, then it is certain that you have never been born again.

2. If you have believed in Christ as your Savior and Lord, you will have the witness of the Holy Spirit that you are a child of God. Romans 8:14-15, "For as many as are led by the Spirit of God, they are the sons of God. For ye have not received the spirit of bondage again to fear; but ye have received the spirit of adoption, whereby we cry, Abba, Father. The Spirit Himself beareth witness with our Spirit that we are the children of God." What could be more clear? Just these verses which are only a few of the many in God's Word reveal the fact that we can KNOW we are saved in this life and that it is God's will for us to KNOW.

3. If you have been born again you will have been cleansed from all sin and delivered from the power and dominion of sin as well

as from the love of sin. (Matt. 1:21b) "He shall save his people FROM their sins." The blood of Jesus Christ cleanseth us from all sin. Notice the present tense in the word CLEANSETH. And "If we confess our sins, he is faithful and just to forgive us our sins, and to cleanse us from all unrighteousness." I John 1:9.

What is salvation --- but the redemption of man from sin and bondage. And when the problem of sin has been cleared away --- the knowledge of being saved NOW is definitely assured.

Think for a moment of the words of Jesus to the disciples in Luke 10:20. "Notwithstanding in this rejoice not, that the spirits are subject unto you; but rather rejoice, because your names are written in heaven."

According to some we would have to say, that Jesus did not know what he was talking about when he spoke these words. Just as Jesus saved men from sin while on earth, so He saves them today and just as He gave the disciples assurance of present salvation so He does today to everyone who will believe His Word. And we know this is true TODAY because God's Word says in Malachi 3:6a "For I am the Lord, I change not;" And the words of the Apostle in Hebrews 13:8 --- "Jesus Christ the same, yesterday and to-day, and forever."

Another instance of Jesus telling the disciples they were saved is in John 15:3. "Now ye are clean through the word which I have spoken unto you." They were clean or cleansed from sin and if cleansed from sin they were saved and knew it. Likewise is it true of any person who will believe and obey the Word of God today.

Another reason some people do not know they are saved or even believe that they can know is because they believe that God has elected only a certain group to salvation and another group to eternal damnation. Hence, they do not know which group they are in until they one day stand before God.

But strange to say such a doctrine is absolutely absent from the pages of God's Word. Rather the clear teaching of God's eternal truth is that "whomsoever" will heed the "Come" (Matt. 11:28) of the Lord Jesus, may be saved and know it in this present life.

RADIO MESSAGE

Walla Walla, Washington
11/01/53
RADIO MESSAGE
PROSSER, WASHINGTON
1/18/59

DIVINE HEALING

The Gospel teaches that forgiveness of sins and healing of the body go hand in hand. If people would receive and believe all the Gospel they would have faith in both healing and forgiveness of sins and could get both at the time of being saved from sin. The following scriptures prove that both benefits were provided in the sacrifices of Calvary: (Matthew 8:17b) "Himself took our infirmities, and bare our sicknesses." "Who his own self bare our sins in His own body on the tree, that we, being dead to sins, should live unto righteousness: by whose stripes ye were healed." (I Peter: 2:24)

Moreover, the following passages prove that both forgiveness of sins and healing of the body should be received at the same time.

"Who forgiveth all thine iniquities; who healeth all thy diseases;" (Psalm 103:3) "For whether is easier, to say, Thy sins be forgiven thee; or to say, Arise, and walk?" (Matthew 9:5). "For this people's heart is waxed gross, and their ears are dull of hearing, and their eyes they have closed; lest at any time they should see with their eyes, and hear with their ears, and should understand with their heart, and should be converted, and I should heal them." (Matthew 13: 15) "Is any sick

36

among you? Let him call for the elders of the church; and let them pray over him, anointing him with oil in the name of the Lord: And the prayer of faith shall save the sick, and the Lord raise him up; and if he have committed sins, they shall be forgiven him." James 5:14-16). Thus, it is very clear that healing is just as easy to receive from God as forgiveness of sins. Both can be received by the same simple faith in God and asking in the name of Jesus. Healing is part of your salvation; so, do not be cheated out of it any more than you permit yourself to be cheated out of forgiveness of sins.

Perhaps it would be well to gain an understanding of just what divine healing is and is not. First, what divine healing is not: it is not healing and health by natural remedies, imagination, will power, personal magnetism, metaphysics, demonology, spiritualism, immunity from death, presumption, and insubordination to God's will, mind over matter, denial of plain facts of sin, sickness, and disease, or natural healing by inherent laws and creative powers in man's body. Second, what divine healing actually is: Divine healing is a definite act of God through faith in Jesus by the power of the Holy Spirit, the Word of God, and the precious blood of Christ whereby the human body is cured, healed, re-paired, delivered from sickness and its power, and made as whole, sound, and healthy as it was before the attack.

There are at least fourteen Hebrew and Greek words found in hundreds of scriptures, which plainly teach the ideas of full salvation, deliverance, preservation, soundness, healing, health, and wholeness of body, soul, and spirit through the gospel. These words are used many times of the body as well as of the soul. Sometimes they are used in the same passages of both body and soul, thus proving that they are not limited to the healing of the soul as some modern Bible students believe.

One of the favorite excuses for unbelief in divine healing today is that healing is not in the atonement because all saints are not healed. One might as well argue that forgiveness of sins is not in the atonement because all sinners are not forgiven. This is an illogical and unscriptural excuse. The reason all Christians are not healed is because they fail to believe that God heals, just like a sinner fails to believe God for the salvation of his soul. Only those who have faith will get what they want. Healing is in the atonement as proved by scripture: "Surely he hath borne our griefs, and carried our sorrows: yet we did esteem him stricken, smitten of God, and afflicted. But he was wounded for our transgressions, he was bruised for our iniquities: the chastisement of our peace was upon him; and with his stripes we are healed." Isaiah 53:4-5.

"When the even was come, they brought unto him many that were possessed with devils: and he cast out the spirits with his word, and healed all that were sick: That it might be fulfilled which was spoken by Esaias the prophet, saying, "Himself took our infirmities, and bare our sicknesses." (Matthew 8:16-17) confer with (I Peter 2:24).

Another excuse for unbelief is the claim that it is not always God's will to heal. This is one of the greatest deceptions and lies of Satan. Note the following: God would not have healed people in both testaments as proved in many cases in Scripture if it had not been his will to heal all who came in faith to him. God is no respecter of persons and he has told us if anyone has a respect of persons he has sinned. This proves that God will heal all alike if he has ever healed anyone. Everyone can be healed the same way that others have been healed and they have the same right to such benefits for which Jesus died.

God would not have made plain his will concerning healing, if it were not his will to always heal those who meet his conditions of healing.

God would have been the originator of sin and sickness, if it had been his will for such to continue in the human race. He would not have healed even one person and he would not have provided for freely promised healing if he were responsible for sickness.

It was God's will that man should be healthy and sinless forever when he created him, and that is still his highest will: "Beloved, I wish above all things that thou mayest prosper and be in health, even as thy soul prospereth." (III John 1:2)

Jesus Christ proved it to be God's will to heal all the sick when he actually healed all that were oppressed of the devil. And when he gave the early church power to carry on the work He "began both to do and teach." Neither Christ nor the early believers would have destroyed sickness as the work of the devil if it had been the work of God.

Sin is also the will of God if sicknesses are, for both were dealt with on the same basis.

Satan and demons would not fight to make and keep men sick if it was the will of God for them to be sick. Satan would try to make men well if it were the will of God for them to be sick. It is an unfailing principle of Satan to do work just the opposite of the will of God. When one argues that it is God's will for them or anyone to be sick he is in co-operation with Satan and not God.

Jesus would not have died to heal men of sickness if it is the will of God for them to be sick, and if he wanted men to bear it.

Sickness is an enemy and death is an enemy, so why should it be God's will that his enemies should be the victor in the lives of his people?

It is as impossible for God to communicate disease as it is for him to communicate and propagate sin and rebellion. Neither sickness, nor sin comes from God for they do not belong to him. They belong to a fallen world of sinful creatures.

If it were not the will of God to always heal he never would have provided the means of healing, made a covenant to heal, promised healing, demonstrated it, rebuked men for not having faith for it, continued to heal in every age, and he never would have made healing a part of the spiritual equipment of the church and proof that an individual is a full believer.

RADIO MESSAGE

Walla Walla, Washington
11/8/53
RADIO MESSAGE
MONETT, MISSOURI
10/11/55
RADIO MESSAGE
PROSSER, WASHINGTON
10/26/58

"SIN AND SALVATION"

"For the wages of sin is death; but the gift of God is eternal life through Jesus Christ our Lord." (Romans 6:23)

The greatest problem and curse in the world today is the curse and problem of sin. The toll which it takes in human life is unequalled by any other power. No other power or influence brings such tragedy as the power and dominion of sin resident in the hearts and lives of sinful men and women, and not only the heartache, sorrow and woe caused by sin in the life; but infinitely more terrible is the sorrow and woe to be suffered by Christ-rejecting men and women in eternity . . .

You may well ask --- "What is the answer, what is the solution to the problem?" The Bible answer --- and the only answer of any real value is --- Solve the greatest problem in the world today – SIN – and you'll solve the problem of crime and vice. Solve the universal problem of sin and you'll drive the war-clouds away from the world horizons in a moment; solve the problem of sin and every strife and contention on the individual level will be cleared away. The primary reason for sorrow and heartache across the world today can ultimately be traced to indwelling sin within the human heart.

But beyond comparison to the present sorrow will be the eternal damnation of never-dying souls simply because they loved their sin more than God. Oh, yes, I know judgment and eternal punishment are not popular subjects; the reason being because people want to live in sin without any worry regarding punishment for their unrighteousness. It would seem that anyone taking a moments time to use an ounce of "common sense" could realize that of necessity sin must not go unpunished. Civil justice very well reveals the likeness and necessity of moral justice. For example --- a man commits a murder and is apprehended for his crime and sentenced. And justly so. Any civil law which is only advisory and does not have a penalty for law-breaking is absolutely no law at all. Likewise, it is true of the moral law of God. God would be unjust to allow sin to go unpunished. Someone may ask, "how can God be just in punishing for eternity the sins committed in a brief life-time on earth?" A man can commit murder in a moment, but he may suffer death or life imprisonment --- therefore it is not the time element involved in the committing of the crime or sin --- but rather the seriousness of the offense.

Our eternal destiny is a matter of life and death --- life if we love and serve God and punishment if we do not.

Let not anyone think God will make a special "pet" out of them and by-pass sin. There aren't any exceptions when it comes to God's laws. God is not a respecter of persons.

The Bible statement --- "Choose ye this day whom ye will serve" still holds true in this 20th century. You have a free-will with which to choose. God will someday balance the books to judge whether you have chosen rightly or not.

The Bible abounds with illustrations of God's judgment upon sin. Noah told the people of his day that judgment was coming but they laughed. Judgment did come and ALL outside the ark perished. Achan thought he could get away with his sin, but God apprehended him and death was his punishment. Annanias and Saphirah of the New Testament church lied to God and they were carried out.

God's Word is still true today --- "The wages of sin is death." And the judgment day no one will be able to evade.

Thank God this not only warns of the awful wages of sin, but also provides a way of escape --- through the Lord Jesus Christ. And notice --- it is the "gift of God". A "gift" ceases to be a gift when any price is paid for it.

Consider the love and mercy of God in giving Jesus Christ as a sacrifice for the sins of the world. Man, the criminal, does not seek God for reconciliation, but God, the person wronged seeks to bring man back to Himself once again. And yet people today say --- "What has God done for me?" When all along He is the One who has gone the "second mile".

The apostle Paul wrote --- "But God commendeth his love toward us, in that, while we were yet sinners, Christ died for us." (Romans 5:8)

And Peter tells us: (II Peter 3:9) "The Lord is not slack concerning his promise, as some men count slackness; but is long-suffering to us-ward, not willing that any should perish, but that all should come to repentance."

In spite of the awfulness of sin --- God has provided a remedy for it through the Lord Jesus Christ; thereby granting eternal life to "whosoever will".

PACKWOOD, WASHINGTON

12/16/62
A.M.

"THE PERFECT GIFT"

Text: "but when the fulness of the time was come, God sent forth his Son, made of a woman, made under the law, To redeem them that were under the law, that we might receive the adoption of sons." (Galatians 4:4-5)

I. INTRODUCTION: "One dark night near 2000 years ago, this world stood poised on the eve of the greatest event in its history. Since its creation, no other single act would have such a far-reaching effect as that about to transpire. For on this night God is about to come to earth – to allow his son Jesus Christ to be born of a woman.

God became man so that he might bring man to God.

So astonishing an event was this that man ever since has been attempting to comprehend its significance. Today, more than 19 centuries later, the majority of men still do not.

But the fact that man does not understand the greatness or kindness of God does not alter the facts - as some foolish men claim it does. For whether or not men believe God does not alter the nature of God or destroy his plan of redemption, God still is. And His plan of redemption is still valid today for all who will believe.

43

II. THE RIGHT TIME: "…when the fullness of time was come".

    A. God's planning and timing were perfect.

        1. At the adoration of the shepherds

            a. "And the angel said unto them, Fear not: for, behold, I bring you good tidings of great joy, which shall be to all people. For unto you is born this day in the city of David a Saviour, which is Christ the Lord." (Luke 2:10-11).

        2. Jesus said in John 16:28, "I came forth from the father and am come into the world…"

    B. But from eternity past this had been the plan of God.

        1. Revelations 13:8 speaks of the "… Lamb slain from the foundation of the world," That is, that the death of Christ which was for-ordained from the foundation of the world, is said to have taken place in the councils of him with whom the end and the beginning are one.

        2. Peter states the same things: "Who verily was foreordained before the foundation of the world, but was manifest in these last times for you." (I Peter 1:20).

        3. This joining together of God and human flesh had been in the eternal councils of God before the foundations of the world.

        4. All Divine-human workings were directed toward this goal.

III. THE RIGHT PERSON: "... GOD SENT FORTH HIS SON..."

A. The golden text of the Bible ... (John 3:16)

    1. His only Son – through the incarnation God (that is, the son of God) became man. This does not mean that either nature was lost – but rather a uniting of both in one.

    2. Only Christ was able to die for the sins of the people.

IV. THE RIGHT WAY: "...: made of a woman, made under the law."

A. "And I will put enmity between thee and the woman, and between thy seed and her seed; it shall bruise thy head, and thou shalt bruise his heel". (Genesis 3:15).

    1. He came by means of the virgin birth and lived a virgin life (perfect sinlessness). The latter as great a miracle as the former. He was born miraculously, lived miraculously, rose from the dead miraculously, and left the world miraculously.

    2. In human flesh he shared the tests of human flesh, yet lived without sin.

B. A savior for both Jews and Gentiles.

V. THE RIGHT PURPOSE: (Galatians 4:5) "To redeem them that were under the law, that we might receive the adoption of sons. "

A. Jesus himself said: "For the Son of man is come to seek and to save that which was lost." (Luke 19:10).

GOD'S LOVE FOR ALL MANKIND

<u>Text:</u> "For God so loved the world, that he gave his only begotten Son, that whosoever believeth in him should not perish, but have everlasting life. For God sent not his Son into the world to condemn the world; but that the world through him might be saved. He that believeth on him is not condemned: but he that believeth not is condemned already, because he hath not believed in the name of the only begotten Son of God." (John 3:16-18)

<u>Also:</u> "For ye know the grace of our Lord Jesus Christ, that, though he was rich, yet for your sakes he became poor, that ye through his poverty might be rich." (II Corinthians 8:9)

<u>And:</u> "For he hath made him to be sin for us, who knew no sin; that we might be made the righteousness of God in him." (II Corinthians 5:21)

<u>Further:</u> "Forasmuch as ye know that ye were not redeemed with corruptible things, as silver and gold, from your vain conversation received by tradition from your fathers; But with the precious blood of Christ, as of a lamb without blemish and without spot: Who verily was foreordained before the foundation of the world, but was manifest in these last times for you, Who by him do believe in God, that raised him up from the dead, and gave him glory; that your faith and hope might be in God." (I Peter 1:18-21)

<u>Again:</u> "And he is the propitiation for our sins: and not for ours only, but also for the sins of the whole world. Hereby perceive we the love of God, because he laid down his life for us: . . . In this was manifested the love of God toward us, because that God sent his only begotten Son into the world, that we might live through him. Herein is love, not that we loved God, but that he loved us, and sent his Son to be the propitiation for our sins." (I John 2:2; 3:16 and 4::9-10)

Propitiation: John is declaring in (I John 2:2) that God has made provision for the whole world, so that no one is excluded from the scope of God's mercy. In other words, God has done His part in providing salvation from sin for all humanity; however, <u>each person</u>

must for himself / herself come to God through Jesus Christ in order to be saved.

Propitiation is that atoning / redemptive work of Christ who bore the just wrath of God upon Himself, thus satisfying the justice of God, so that all who come to Him might find life in Christ. Because Jesus Christ has borne the just penalty of sin which is death, God is able to show mercy and still be just and therefore the justifier of all who believe in Jesus Christ.

Like as a father pitieth his children, so the Lord pitieth them that fear him.

For he knoweth our frame; he remembereth that we are dust.

As for man, his days are as grass: as a flower of the field, so he flourisheth.

For the wind passeth over it, and it is gone; and the place thereof shall know it no more.

But the mercy of the LORD is from everlasting to everlasting upon them that fear him, and his righteousness unto children's children; (Psalms 103:13-17)

GOD'S MERCY FOR ALL WHO CALL

GRACE --- God GIVING us that which we DO NOT deserve; whereas MERCY is God NOT GIVING us that which we DO deserve.

MERCY has been defined further as, a form of love determined by the state or condition of its object, which state is one of suffering and need while they may be unworthy or undeserving.

Scripture declares what God is like; i.e. His character. CONSIDER: To Moses on Mount Sinai the Bible records: "And the LORD passed by before him, and proclaimed, The LORD, The LORD God, merciful and gracious, longsuffering, and abundant in goodness and truth, Keeping mercy for thousands, forgiving iniquity and transgression and sin, and that will by no means clear the guilty; visiting the iniquity of the fathers upon the children, and upon the children's children, unto the third and to the fourth generation." (Exodus 34:6, 7)

"(For the LORD thy God is a merciful God;) he will not forsake thee, neither destroy thee, nor forget the covenant of thy fathers which he sware unto them." Deuteronomy 4:31 and ... again ---"Also unto thee, O Lord, belongeth mercy: for thou renderest to every man according to his work." (Psalms 62:12)

Moreover: "Who is a God like unto thee, that pardoneth iniquity, and passeth by the transgression of the remnant of his heritage? he retaineth not his anger forever, because he delighteth in mercy. . . Thou wilt perform the truth to Jacob, and the mercy to Abraham, which thou hast sworn unto our fathers from the days of old." (Micah 7:18, 20)

The prophet Jeremiah spoke to the Jewish exiles in Babylon and encouraged them with these words: "For thus saith the LORD, That after seventy years be accomplished at Babylon I will visit you, and perform my good word toward you, in causing you to return to this place. For I know the thoughts that I think toward you, saith the LORD, thoughts of peace, and not of evil, to give you an expected end." (Jeremiah 29:10, 11)

The Psalmist declared: "The LORD is merciful and gracious, slow to anger, and plenteous in mercy.

He hath not dealt with us after our sins; nor rewarded us according to our iniquities.

For as the heaven is high above the earth, so great is his mercy toward them that fear him.

But the mercy of the Lord is from everlasting to everlasting upon them that fear him, and his righteousness unto children's children;

To such as keep his covenant, and to those that remember his commandments to do them." (Psalms 103:8, 10, 11, 17, 18)

Illustration: A mother pleading for her son because he had fallen asleep at his sentry duty in time of war. Justice declared he was to be shot. However, she was not asking for justice, but for mercy.

The first commandment states: "Thou shalt have no other gods before me. . . Thou shalt not bow down thyself to them, nor serve them: for I the Lord thy God am a jealous God, visiting the iniquity of the fathers upon the children unto the third and fourth generation of them that hate me; And showing mercy unto thousands of them that love me, and keep my commandments." (Exodus 20:3, 5, 6)

Further: "It is of the LORD's mercies that we are not consumed, because his compassions fail not. They are new every morning: great is thy faithfulness." (Lamentations 3:22, 23)

THE CHRISTIAN IS TO BE LIKE HIS LORD — Consider: the following:

The Psalmist declared: "With the merciful thou wilt show thyself merciful." (Psalms 18:25a)

Jesus said: "Blessed are the merciful: for they shall obtain mercy;" (Matthew 5:7) . . . And again: "Be ye therefore merciful, as your Father also is merciful." (Luke 6:36)

Then the Apostle Paul exhorted: "Forbearing one another, and forgiving one another, if any man have a quarrel against any: even as Christ forgave you, so also do ye." (Colossians 3:13)

"And be ye kind one to another, tenderhearted, forgiving one another, even as God for Christ's sake hath forgiven you." (Ephesians 4:32)

MAN'S RESPONSIBILITY IN ORDER TO RECEIVE GOD's SALVATION

I. ". . . Believe on the Lord Jesus Christ, and thou shalt be saved. . ." (Acts 16:31)

II. Confession of sin: "If we confess our sins, he is faithful and just to forgive us our sins, and to cleanse us from all unrighteousness." (I John 1:9)

III. John the Baptist and Jesus as well as the apostles came declaring the human requirement of repentance in order to be saved.

    1. Repentance is that change of heart and mind whereby we are willing to admit our need of God with a willingness to change.

IV. Jesus declared the greatest commandment of all is to LOVE THE LORD THY GOD. "Thou shalt love the Lord thy God with all thy heart, and with all thy soul, and with all thy mind. This is the first and great commandment." (Matthew 22:37a - 38)

V. **What does it mean to love God?**

    1. The Psalmist declared: "Ye that love the Lord, hate evil:"(Psalms 97:10a)

    2. Again the Psalmist declared: "Thy throne, O God, is for ever and ever: the sceptre of thy kingdom is a right sceptre. Thou lovest righteousness, and hatest wickedness: . . ." (Psalms 45:6-7a) Jesus fulfilled these prophetic words: "But unto the Son he saith, Thy throne, O God, is for ever and ever: a sceptre of righteousness is the sceptre of thy kingdom. Thou hast loved righteousness, and hated iniquity; . . ." (Hebrews 1:8-9a)

3. Love—more than emotion—though there is an emotional aspect—love is action, doing, obedience to the word and will of God.

CONCLUSION: When God in Christ has done so much for us, how can we not be willing to be devoted to Him and love Him with all our hearts? It was Jesus who asked Peter: "Simon Peter, Simon, son of Jonas, lovest thou me . . ?" Three times he asked the same question. Each time, Jesus gave him something to do---"Feed my lambs," feed my sheep." (John 21:15-17) When Jesus called His disciples, the call was simple, yet emphatic: "Follow me." In verse 19, Jesus commanded Peter, "Follow me." Followed by, in verse 22, "follow thou me." (John 21:22b)

Who redeemeth thy life from destruction; who crowneth thee with lovingkindness and tender mercies;

Who satisfieth thy mouth with good things; so that thy youth is renewed like the eagle's. (Psalm 103:4-5)

He hath not dealt with us after our sins; nor rewarded us according to our iniquities.

For as the heaven is high above the earth, so great is his mercy toward them that fear him.

As far as the east is from the west, so far hath he removed our transgressions from us. (Psalm 103:10-12)

THE FEAR OF GOD

TEXT: "Let us hear the conclusion of the whole matter: Fear God, and keep his commandments: for this is the whole duty of man." (Ecclesiastes 12:13)

INTRODUCTION: What does the "fear of God" mean? Does it mean that humans are to run and hide from God---try to somehow prevent God from seeing them? No, never does the "fear of God" as used in Holy Scripture ever mean to run **from** God---just the opposite, it means to run **to** God and bow before Him! To attempt hiding from God is fruitless, for God's Word declares: **"Neither is there any creature that is not manifest in his sight: but all things are naked and opened unto the eyes of him with whom we have to do." (Hebrews 4:13)**

Biblical fear of God always means that humanity is to have a reverence and respect for God in order that we may love, obey and serve Him acceptably with reverence and godly fear. "Wherefore we receiving a kingdom which cannot be moved, let us have grace, whereby we may serve God acceptably with reverence and godly fear:" (Hebrews 12:28) In other words, the true fear of God is a positive virtue enabling us to please God and obey Him and keep His commandments.

I. THE FEAR OF GOD JOINED TO ACTION / DOING:

A. **"O that there were such an heart in them, that they would fear me, and keep all my commandments always, that it might be well with them, and with their children forever!"** (Deuteronomy 5:29)

    (1.) Note the Divine **longing** for human response to God that He might bless them!

B. "Now these are the commandments, the statutes, and the judgments, which the LORD your God commanded to teach you, that ye might do them in the land whither ye go to possess it: (Deuteronomy 6:1)

    (2) "That thou mightest fear the LORD thy God, to keep all his statutes and his commandments, which I command thee, thou, and thy son, and thy son's son, all the days of thy life; and that thy days may be prolonged. (Deuteronomy 6:2)

    (3) "Hear therefore, O Israel, and observe to do it; that it may be well with thee, . . ." (Deuteronomy 6:3a) The command again: "Thou shalt fear the Lord thy God, and serve him, . . ." (Deuteronomy 6:13a)

C. "And now, Israel, what doth the LORD thy God require of thee, but to fear the LORD thy God, to walk in all his ways, and to love him, and to serve the LORD thy God with all thy heart and with all thy soul, To keep the commandments of the LORD, and his statutes, which I command thee this day for thy good?" (Deuteronomy 10:12-13)

    1. The prophet Micah questions and then gives the answer: "Wherewith shall I come before the LORD, and bow myself before the high God? shall I come before him with burnt offerings, with calves of a year old? (7) Will the LORD be pleased with thousands of rams, or with ten thousands of rivers of oil? shall I give my firstborn for my transgression, the fruit of my body for the sin of my soul? (8) He hath shewed thee, O man, what is good; and what doth the LORD require of thee, but to do justly, and to love mercy, and to walk humbly with thy God?" (Micah 6:6-8)

D. God spoke to Joshua these words: "Now therefore fear the LORD, and serve him in sincerity and truth: and put away the gods which your fathers served on the other side of the flood, and in Egypt; and serve ye the LORD." (Joshua 24:14)

E. The Psalmist declared: "The fear of the LORD is clean, enduring for ever: the judgments of the LORD are true and righteous altogether." (Psalm 19:9)

II. PROMISED BLESSNGS TO THOSE WHO FEAR GOD:

A. The Psalmist declares: " . . . he honoureth them that fear the LORD . . ." (Psalm 15:4b)

1. "Oh how great is thy goodness, which thou hast laid up for them that fear thee; which thou hast wrought for them that trust in thee before the sons of men!" (Psalm 31:19)
2. "Behold, the eye of the LORD is upon them that fear him, upon them that hope in his mercy; To deliver their soul from death, and to keep them alive in famine." (Psalms 33:18-19)
3. "Surely his salvation is nigh them that fear him; that glory may dwell in our land." (Psalms 85:9)
4. "Like as a father pitieth his children, so the LORD pitieth them that fear him. For he knoweth our frame; he remembereth that we are dust." (Psalms 103:13-14)
5. "Ye that fear the LORD, trust in the LORD: he is their help and their shield. He will bless them that fear the Lord, both small and great." (Psalms 115:11, 13)
6. " . . . Ye that fear the LORD, bless the LORD." (Psalms 135:20b)
7. "The Lord taketh pleasure in them that fear him, in those that hope in his mercy." (Psalms 147:11)
8. "The fear of the LORD prolongeth days: but the years of the wicked shall be shortened." (Proverbs 10:27)

9. "In the fear of the LORD is strong confidence: and his children shall have a place of refuge." (Proverbs 14:26)
10. "The fear of the LORD tendeth to life: and he that hath it shall abide satisfied; he shall not be visited with evil." (Proverbs 19:23)

III. CONCLUSION: JESUS' ADMONITION TO FEAR THE LIVING GOD:

A. "And I say unto you my friends, Be not afraid of them that kill the body, and after that have no more that they can do. But I will forewarn you whom ye shall fear: Fear him, which after he hath killed hath power to cast into hell; yea, I say unto you, Fear him." (Luke 12:4-5)

HUNGERING & THIRSTING AFTER GOD

SCRIPTURE: "As the hart panteth after the water brooks, so panteth my soul after thee, O God. (2) My soul thirsteth for God, for the living God: when shall I come and appear before God?" (Psalms 42:1, 2)

"O God, thou art my God; early will I seek thee: my soul thirsteth for thee, my flesh longeth for thee in a dry and thirsty land, where no water is;" (Psalms 63:1)

"How amiable are thy tabernacles, O LORD of hosts! (2) My soul longeth, yea, even fainteth for the courts of the LORD: my heart and my flesh crieth out for the living God." (Psalms 84:1, 2)

"Blessed are they which do hunger and thirst after righteousness: for they shall be filled." (Matthew 5:6)

I. ONLY THE LIVING GOD CAN FILL THE LONGING IN THE HUMAN HEART:

    A. A wise man once said: "Thou hast made us for Thyself, and our hearts are restless till they find rest in Thee."

        1. Only God can meet the need of the human heart.

    B. When sin entered the human family, mankind became separated from the very source of life, joy and happiness.

II. HOW MAY WE FIND AND ENJOY THE LIVING GOD?:

    A. Illus. of the religious leader in India. . .

        1. Do we / you hunger and thirst after God? Do we / you hunger and thirst after God?

B. Notice that the thirst to fill the emptiness within the heart has only ONE source from which to be satisfied.

   1. The Psalmist declared that he thirsted after GOD! Not religion, nor mere ceremony or anything else for only God Himself can satisfy the longing within the human heart.

C. Scripture admonishes us to SEEK after / for God

   1. Fellowship, communion with the living God!
   2. "But seek ye first the kingdom of God, and his righteousness; and all these things shall be added unto you." (Matthew 6:33)
   3. God will not force Himself on anyone; however, He always responds to a hungry, thirsting heart.

THE PERSON AND SACRIFICIAL DEATH OF "JESUS CHRIST" FOLLOWED BY THE RESURRECTION

I. JESUS CHRIST THE SON OF GOD

   A. "For God so loved the world, that he gave his only begotten Son, that whosoever believeth in him should not perish, but have everlasting life." (John 3:16)

      1. " The Jews answered him, saying, For a good work we stone thee not; but for blasphemy; and because that thou, being a man, makest thyself God." . . . To the Jews Jesus said, "Say ye of him, whom the Father hath sanctified, and sent into the world, Thou blasphemest; because I said, I am the Son of God?" (John 10:33, 36)

      2. "For he hath made him to be sin for us, who knew no sin; that we might be made the righteousness of God in him." (II Corinthians 5:21)

      3. "Who did no sin, neither was guile found in his mouth: . . . (24) Who his own self bare our sins in his own body on the tree, that we, being dead to sins, should live unto righteousness: by whose stripes ye were healed." (I Peter 2:22, 24)

      4. "Neither is there salvation in any other: for there is none other name under heaven given among men, whereby we must be saved." (Acts 4:12)

   B. Though fully human, yet Jesus Christ was also GOD! GOD revealed or manifested in human form---just as fully human as any one of us---yet also GOD!

1. Scripture declares that Jesus was also GOD. "In the beginning was the Word, and the Word was with God, and the Word was God." (John 1:1)
2. Following the resurrection Thomas said, "And Thomas answered and said unto him, My Lord and my God." (John 20:28)

II. THE BODILY RESURRECTION OF JESUS CHRIST:

A. I Corinthians 15:1ff.

1. While Jesus Christ had to die for the sins of the world in order to provide potential salvation for all---we celebrated "Good Friday" just last week in memory of that event---nonetheless it is also true that without the resurrection of Jesus Christ there would be no salvation for anyone!

   a. Paul the Apostle declares in I Corinthians 15:14 "And if Christ be not risen, then is our preaching vain, and your faith is also vain." Simply stated, if Jesus did not rise from the dead, there is no salvation and life for anyone! For Paul goes on to say, "And if Christ be not raised, your faith is vain; ye are yet in your sins." (I Corinthians 15:17)
   b. "But now is Christ risen from the dead, and become the firstfruits of them that slept." (Verse 20)

B. The resurrection of Jesus Christ was not a hidden event. ". . . he was seen of Cephas, then of the twelve: After that, he was seen of above five hundred brethren at once; of whom the greater part remain unto this present, but some are fallen asleep. After that, he was seen of James; then of all the apostles. And last of all he was seen of me also, as of one born out of due time." (I Corinthians 15:5-8)

1. Paul again declared: "For I delivered unto you first of all that which I also received, how that Christ died for our sins according to the Scriptures; And that he was buried, and that he rose again the third day according to the Scriptures:" (I Corinthians 15:3, 4)

   a. God's written word prophetically declared the death, burial, and resurrection of our Lord Jesus Christ. GOD FULFILLED HIS WORD IN EVERY EVENT CONCERNING OUR LORD JESUS CHRIST!

III. THE BELIEVER'S RESURRECTION GUARANTEED:

A. "For since by man came death, by man came also the resurrection of the dead . . . Behold, I shew you a mystery; We shall not all sleep, but we shall all be changed, In a moment, in the twinkling of an eye, at the last trump: for the trumpet shall sound, and the dead shall be raised incorruptible, and we shall be changed. For this corruptible must put on incorruption, and this mortal must put on immortality. So, when this corruptible shall have put on incorruption, and this mortal shall have put on immortality, then shall be brought to pass the saying that is written, Death is swallowed up in victory. O death, where is thy sting? O grave, where is thy victory? The sting of death is sin; and the strength of sin is the law. But thanks be to God, which giveth us the victory through our Lord Jesus Christ. Therefore, my beloved brethren, be ye steadfast, unmoveable, always abounding in the work of the Lord, forasmuch as ye know that your labour is not in vain in the Lord." (I Corinthians 15:21; 51-58)

The glory of the LORD shall endure for ever: the LORD shall rejoice in his works.

He looketh on the earth, and it trembleth: he toucheth the hills, and they smoke.

I will sing unto the LORD as long as I live: I will sing praise to my God while I have my being.

My meditation of him shall be sweet: I will be glad in the LORD. (Psalms 104:31-34)

PARABLE OF THE GOOD SAMARITAN

TEXT: Luke 10:25-37

INTRODUCTION: Originally the Samaritans came from colonists brought in from Assyria to repopulate the land after Israel had been conquered by Assyria. Perhaps due to inter-marriage between the Samaritans and the Jews, joined with a mixing of heathen worship with Judaism, there had developed a hatred between the Jews and Samaritans. Thus, Jesus' parable was a perfect background for teaching "love to your neighbor". Therefore, nationality or race, color of skin or language should never prevent us from doing good to someone in need.

II. LOVE TO / FOR GOD AND LOVE TO / FOR OUR NEIGHBOR:

A. A "lawyer" stood up trying to tempt him saying, (lit.) "By doing what shall I inherit eternal life?" Emphasis is on "doing" by this lawyer. This lawyer was trying to trick or trap Jesus.

1. Jesus asked the lawyer, "What is written in the law? How readest thou?"
2. The lawyer answered by quoting from the law with which he was very familiar.

a. "Thou shalt love the Lord thy God with all thy heart, and with all thy soul, and with all thy strength, and with all thy mind; and thy neighbor as thyself."

3. Jesus answered, "Thou hast answered right: this do, and thou shalt live."

a. The problem is that "no one" has ever kept the "law" – for to break "one" commandment is to

break them all. Only by receiving and knowing /
obeying Jesus Christ can we ever hope to fulfill
the law of God – in His strength and by His grace!
b. "But he, willing to justify himself, said unto Jesus,
And who is my neighbor?"
c. This lawyer thought he had found an escape for
himself as the Jews "split hairs" over this question
and exclude from "neighbor" Gentiles and
especially "Samaritans".

III. <u>JESUS' PARABLE OF THE GOOD SAMARITAN</u>:

A. Vs. 30 – "A certain man went down from Jerusalem to
Jericho, and fell among thieves, which stripped him of his
raiment, and wounded him, and departed, leaving him
half dead." Thieves and robbers beat and robbed this man,
leaving him half dead.

   1. Vs. 31 – "And by chance there came down a certain
   priest that way: and when he saw him, he passed by
   on the other side."

      a. This was a vivid and powerful picture of the vice
      of Jewish ceremonial cleanliness at the cost of
      moral principle and duty.

   2. Vs. 32 – The Levite behaved precisely as the priest had
   done and for the same reason.

B. Vs. 33 – "But a certain Samaritan, as he journeyed, came
where he was: and when he saw him, he had compassion
on him, Vs.34. And went to him, and bound up his wounds,
pouring in oil and wine, and set him on his own beast, and
brought him to an inn, and took care of him. Vs. 35 And
on the morrow when he departed, he took out two pence,

and gave them to the host, and said unto him, Take care of him; and whatsoever thou spendest more, when I come again, I will repay thee."

1. Of all people to do a neighborly act! And at his own expense with no possibility of being repaid! He cared for him over night, paid for his keep until his return. A classic example of caring and compassion upon a "stranger".

2. Jesus' question to the lawyer who had sought to justify himself: Vs. 36 "Which now of these three, thinkest thou, was neighbor unto him that fell among the thieves?" Jesus challenges the lawyer with a question having an obvious answer. **Which of the three – priest, Levite, or Samaritan was neighbor to this traveler in need?**

   a. The lawyer's response: "And he said, He that showed mercy on him."

3. Jesus' application of the parable to this lawyer, V. 37 – "Go, and do thou likewise."

III. <u>CONCLUSION</u>: This parable of the Good Samaritan has built the world's hospitals and, if understood and practiced, will remove race prejudice, national hatred and war, as well as class jealousy.

A living faith in God joined with obedience to the Word and will of God is required of all who would be followers of Jesus Christ. Relationship with God is more than lip-service or mere formality – it is life, living out that which we profess to believe. Someone has well said, "If Christianity is not practical, it is not Biblical Christianity."

It was the Apostle James who said, "But be ye doers of the word, and not hearers only, deceiving your own selves." (James 1:22)

Bless the LORD, O my soul. Oh LORD my God, thou art very great; thou art clothed with honour and majesty.

Who coverest thyself with light as with a garment: who stretchest out the heavens like a curtain:

Who layeth the beams of his chambers in the waters: who maketh the clouds his chariot: who walketh upon the wings of the wind:

Who maketh his angels spirits; his ministers a flaming fire:

Who laid the foundations of the earth, that it should not be removed for ever. (Psalm 104:1-5)

1/22/06 – MOUNTAIN VIEW
RETIREMENT CENTER – 3:30 P.M.

THE DIVINE INVITATION

TEXT: "Come unto me, all ye that labour and are heavy laden, and I will give you rest. Take my yoke upon you, and learn of me; for I am meek and lowly in heart: and ye shall find rest unto your souls. For my yoke is easy, and my burden is light." (Matthew 11:28-30)

I. INTRODUCTION: The entire Bible is a revelation of the living God seeking fellowship and a living relationship with humanity, His crowning creative work. From Genesis, the first book of the bible, to Revelation, the last book of the bible, it is a story of God seeking man. In the Garden of Eden, it was not Adam and Eve running to God after they had disobeyed His clear and direct command. Rather, they hid from God until He came seeking them. Sin had separated man from God and the close fellowship they once had was broken. Did Adam and Eve seek the restoration of fellowship and a close walk with God? No, it was God, the offended One, who moved to restore fellowship with His creation. And it is still so today. It is God who seeks to bring disobedient mankind back to Himself. In order to restore the desired relationship God took the most drastic measure possible. He gave His only begotten Son as a sacrifice to bring humanity back to Himself.

II. THE INVITATION OF GOD THROUGH THE PROPHET ISAIAH:

A. "Come now, and let us reason together, saith the LORD: though your sins be as scarlet, they shall be as white as snow; though they be red like crimson, they shall be as wool. If ye be willing and obedient, ye shall eat the good of the land:" (Isaiah 1:18, 19)

   1. This is a picture of God calling His chosen people, Israel, back to Himself. Though God was and is the offended One, He moves to bring the sinning nation or the sinner back to Himself.
   2. Again, the prophet speaks for God: "Incline your ear, and come unto me: hear, and your soul shall live; . . ." (Isaiah 55:3a)

III. JESUS CHRIST INVITES FALLEN HUMANITY TO COME TO HIM:

A. (Our text) "Come unto me . . ."

   1. Also: When Jesus was at a Jewish feast in Jerusalem, He cried out: "If any man thirst, let him come unto me and drink." (John 7:37b)
   2. Again: Jesus, the good shepherd, speaking to the Jews and to whoever would listen,

"I am come that they might have life, and that they might have it more abundantly." (John 10:10b)

IV. THE LAST INVITATION:

A. "And the Spirit and the bride say, Come. And let him that heareth say, Come. And let him that is athirst come. And whosoever will, let him take the water of life freely." (Revelation 22:17)

GOD'S WILL AND MAN'S WILL

A fundamental principle and all Divine / human relationships can be simply stated as "God's part" and "man's part" or "God working" and "man working." God is in control of all things yet leaves men free to either cooperate with the Divine will or reject that will. Holy Scripture abounds with examples demonstrating this is reality.

From Adam onward, the door for all human cooperation with the purpose and plan of God has been open. Result? Obedience always has and always will bring God's blessing whereas disobedience or rejection of the Divine will produces heartache and misery.

While God longs for a fellowship with his crowning act of creation – man – He has endowed man with a free will. We can exercise our will and choose God's way or choose to reject His Lordship over our lives. This is the risk God took when he created us with the power of free will. The living God never uses coercion. He speaks, woos, and brings circumstances designed to persuade a right decision but he never forces anyone to obey and serve him.

Man and woman were a special creation of God. Though man was created in the image of God he is not Divine: God is the creator and man is totally dependent upon him. While God is the creator and sustainer of all his creation. He nonetheless has chosen to relate to man in a personal way. It is awesome to think the living eternal God who is perfect and complete in Himself – seeks fellowship with his creation.

It is God who seeks man and in a certain sense limits himself by having man work with him. What a blessed privilege.

Mountain View Retirement Home - 05/28/06

<u>WHOSOEVER WILL MAY COME</u>

TEXT: "For God so loved the world, that he gave his only begotten Son, that whosoever believeth in him should not perish, but have everlasting life." (John 3:16)

INTRODUCTION: This verse is often referred to as the "Golden Text" of the Bible. It is so simple; so all-inclusive, so simple. Yet it reveals the heart and desire of the living God. Our emphasis now is on that word, "whosoever." This word declares an open invitation to all, to everyone, none excluded. Consider other Scriptural declarations giving the same wonderful opportunity to share in the life which is in Christ Jesus.

I. THE WORLD INCLUDED IN THIS "WHOSOEVER" INVITATION:

    A. "For God sent not his Son into the world to condemn the world; but that the world through him might be saved." (John 3:17)

        1. "He that believeth on him is not condemned: but he that believeth not is condemned already, because he hath not believed in the name of the only begotten Son of God." (John 3:18)

        2. To the Samaritan woman in Sychar Jesus said, "Jesus answered and said unto her, Whosoever drinketh of

this water shall thirst again: But whosoever drinketh of the water that I shall give him shall never thirst; but the water that I shall give him shall be in him a well of water springing up into everlasting life." (John 4:13, 14)

3. On another occasion Jesus cried out, "If any man thirst, let him come unto me, and drink." (John 7:37b) NOTE especially the word, "any man" or "any person."

4. Another open invitation, "Jesus saith unto him, I am the way, the truth, and the life: no man cometh unto the Father, but by me." (John 14:6)

5. Another "open" invitation by our Lord, "Come unto me, all ye that labour and are heavy laden, and I will give you rest." (Matthew 11:28)

II. AN OPEN INVITATION ALSO IN THE OLD TESTAMENT:

A. The Divine question to all mankind: "Have I any pleasure at all that the wicked should die? saith the Lord God: and not that he should return from his ways, and live?" (Ezekiel 18:23)

1. "Cast away from you all your transgressions, whereby ye have transgressed; and make you a new heart and a new spirit: for why will ye die, O house of Israel? For I have no pleasure in the death of him that dieth, saith the Lord God: wherefore turn yourselves, and live ye." (Ezekiel 18:31, 32)

2. Again: "Say unto them, As I live, saith the Lord God, I have no pleasure in the death of the wicked; but that the wicked turn from his way and live: turn ye, turn ye from your evil ways; for why will ye die, O house of Israel?" (Ezekiel 33:11)

III. <u>THE APOSTOLIC INVITATION:</u>

A. The Apostle Paul declares, "For whosoever shall call upon the name of the Lord shall be saved." (Romans 10:13)

1. "And it shall come to pass, that whosoever shall call on the name of the Lord shall be saved." (Acts 2:21)

B. The Bible ends with the last "whosoever" call: "And the Spirit and the the bride say, Come. And let him that heareth say, Come. And let him that is athirst come. And whosoever will, let him take the water of life freely." (Revelation 22:17)

07/23/06 -- Hearthstone Cottage -- Ellensburg, WA 98926

JESUS CHRIST, THE GOOD SHEPHERD

TEXT: John 10:1-18

I. <u>METAPHORS DESCRIBING OUR WONDERFUL LORD</u>:

A. "I am the door of the sheep:" (John 10:7). "I am the door:" (John 10:9)

1. "I am the good shepherd: . . ." (John 10:11 and 14)
2. "I am the way, the truth, and the life: no man cometh unto the Father, but by me." (John 14:6b)
3. "I am the bread of life: he that cometh to me shall never hunger; and he that believeth on me shall never thirst." (John 6:35b) "I am that bread of life." (John 6:48)
4. "I am the resurrection, and the life: he that believeth in me, though he were dead, yet shall he live: And whosoever liveth and believeth in me shall never die. Believest thou this?" (John 11:25b, 26)
5. "I am Alpha and Omega, the beginning and the ending, . . ." (Revelation 1:8, 11)
6. "Fear not; I am the first and the last." (Revelation 1:17b)

7. "I am he that liveth, and was dead; and, behold, I am alive forevermore," (Rev. 1:18a)

8. "I am Alpha and Omega, the beginning and the end, the first and the last." (Revelation 22:13)

9. "I am the root and the offspring of David, and the bright and morning star." (Revelation 22:16b)

II. THE GOOD SHEPHERD GIVETH HIS LIFE FOR THE SHEEP:

A. "Therefore doth my Father love me, because I lay down my life, that I might take it again. No man taketh it from me, but I lay it down of myself. I have power to lay it down, and I have power to take it again. This commandment have I received of my Father." (John 10:17, 18)

   1. The Bible is clear; Jesus Christ gave Himself, laid down His life for us, that whosoever will may come and be saved.

      a. ". . . I lay down my life for the sheep." (John 10:15b)

B. ". . . he calleth his own sheep by name, and leadeth them out:" (John 10:3b)

   1. ". . . the sheep follow him: for they know his voice. And a stranger will they not follow, but will flee from him: for they know not the voice of strangers." (John 10:4b, 5)

III. DO YOU KNOW THE VOICE OF THE GOOD SHEPHERD?

He sendeth the springs into the valleys, which run among the hills.

They give drink to every beast of the field: the wild assess quench their thirst.

By them shall the fowls of the heaven have their habitation, which sing among the branches:

He watereth the hills from his chambers: the earth is satisfied with the fruit of thy works.

He causeth the grass to grow for the cattle, and herb for the service of man: that he may bring forth food out of the earth; (Psalm 104:10-14)

CHOOSE YOU THIS DAY & CLING TO THE LORD

Text: "And if it seem evil unto you to serve the Lord, **choose you this day whom ye will serve**; whether the gods which your fathers served that were on the other side of the flood, or the gods of the Amorites, in whose land ye dwell: but as for me and my house, we will serve the Lord." (Joshua 24:15)

"I call heaven and earth to record this day against you, that I have set before you life and death, blessing and cursing: therefore **choose** life, that both thou and thy seed may live:"

"That thou mayest love the LORD thy God, and that thou mayest obey his voice, and that thou mayest **cleave** unto him: **for he is thy life**, and the length of thy days: that thou mayest dwell in the land which the LORD sware unto thy fathers, to Abraham, to Isaac, and to Jacob, to give them." (Deuteronomy 30:19, 20)

I. **INTRODUCTION:** The living God has endowed humanity with the power of "free will" or the ability to "choose" or "decide / make a decision". God has no desire to have a relationship with mere "robots"; but He does long for a vital living relationship with creatures made in His image. Though marred by sin, nonetheless humanity has retained the ability to hear, to know, and to understand the Divine call for fellowship with the living God. Moreover, there is no <u>neutral ground</u> in a relationship with God. We are either for HIM or we are against Him.

II. **AN ILLUSTRATION FROM THE LIFE / MINISTRY OF JESUS:**

A. "O Jerusalem, Jerusalem, thou that killest the prophets, and stonest them which are sent unto thee, how often would I have gathered thy children together, even as a hen gathereth her chickens under her wings, and ye would not!" (Matthew 23:37)

1. These words of Jesus establish two truths or principles:

    a. The deep desire of the living God for fellowship and relationship with humanity and,
    b. God will not FORCE people to love and follow Him! We have the choice to either follow Jesus Christ or reject Him.

2. The invitation of our Lord to ALL, everyone, illustrates the freedom of the human will to either accept or reject the Divine invitation.

    a. "Come unto me, all ye that labour and are heavy laden, and I will give you rest. Take my yoke upon you, and learn of me; for I am meek and lowly in heart: and ye shall find rest unto your souls. For my yoke is easy, and my burden is light." (Matthew 11:28-30)
    b. "And the Spirit and the bride say, Come. And let him that heareth say, Come. And let him that is athirst come. And whosoever will, let him take the water of life freely." (Revelation 22:17)
    c. "But whosoever drinketh of the water that I shall give him shall never thirst; but the water that I shall give him shall be in him a well of water springing up into everlasting life." (John 4:14)

III. THE INVITATION TO PARTAKE OF EVERLASTING LIFE CAN ONLY BE ANSWERED BY EACH INDIVIDUAL PERSONALLY:

A. The Roman governor, Pilate, centuries ago asked the Jewish leaders who had brought Jesus before him, (the Jews requested that Barabbas should be released); Pilate asked, **"What shall I do then with Jesus which is called Christ?** They all say unto him, Let him be crucified." (Matthew 27:22b)

1. This is the issue before every human being. "Neither is there salvation in any other: for there is none other name under heaven given among men, whereby we must be saved." (Acts 4:12)

GOD'S PERFECT KNOWLEDGE OF EVERY HUMAN BEING

TEXT: Psalms 139:1-7ff

I. Vs. 1-7 - The living God knows all / everything there is to know about each and every person. Nothing is hid from His eyes.

    A. Consider: "For the word of God is quick, and powerful, and sharper than any two-edged sword, piercing even to the dividing asunder of soul and spirit, and of the joints and marrow, and is a discerner of the thoughts and intents of the heart. Neither is there any creature that is not manifest in his sight: but all things are naked and opened unto the eyes of him with whom we have to do." (Hebrews 4:12, 13)

        1. And thou, Solomon my son, know thou the God of thy father, and serve him with a perfect heart and with a willing mind: for the Lord searcheth all hearts, and understandeth all the imaginations of the thoughts: if thou seek him, he will be found of thee; but if thou forsake him, he will cast thee off forever." (I Chronicles 28:9)

II. THE ATTITUDE OF THE PERSON WHO LONGS TO BE RIGHT WITH GOD AND GOD'S CONCERN FOR EACH ONE:

    A. Vs. 23, 24 "Search me, O God, and know my heart: try me, and know my thoughts: And see if there be any wicked way in me, and lead me in the way everlasting." (Psalms 139:23, 24)

    1. Also: "And they put away the strange gods from among them, and served the LORD: and his soul was grieved for the misery of Israel." (Judges 10:16)

        a. God is grieved and pained because of the misery of humans due to their sinfulness.

        b. Jesus wept over the city of Jerusalem because of their sin which He knew would result in their destruction. (Luke 19:41ff) cf. "O Jerusalem, Jerusalem, thou that killest the prophets, and stonest them which are sent unto thee, how often would I have gathered thy children together, even as a hen gathereth her chickens under her wings, and ye would not." (Matthew 23:37)

III. THE DIVINE LONGING TO SAVE EVERY PERSON FROM SIN AND DESTRUCTION:

  A. The Bible is filled with promises applicable to every human being:

    1. John 3:16, John 10:10, Matthew 11:28-30, and - "And the Spirit and the bride say, Come. And let him that heareth say, Come. And let him that is athirst come. And whosoever will, let him take the water of life freely." (Revelation 22:17)

THE PAIN OF GOD OR THE SUFFERING OF GOD

TEXT: "In all their affliction he was afflicted, and the angel of his presence saved them: in his love and in his pity he redeemed them; and he bare them, and carried them all the days of old." (Isaiah 63:9)

INTRODUCTION: Too often many people think of God as so far above and greater than mere human beings, that therefore He has no feelings or emotions. However, the Bible teaches otherwise. God not only sees but feels our pain, our grief, our distress or on the other hand, our joy and delight. He is not only grieved at the wickedness in a sinful world but as the "heavenly Father" of all believers He feels our pain and distress as well. The Psalmist declares, "Like as a father pitieth his children, so the LORD pitieth them that fear him. For he knoweth our frame; he remembereth that we are dust." (Psalms 103:13, 14)

A. GOD SUFFERS PAIN BECAUSE PEOPLE SIN:

A. "And God saw that the wickedness of man was great in the earth, and that every imagination of the thoughts of his heart was only evil continually. And it repented the LORD that he had made man on the earth, and it grieved him at his heart." (Genesis 6:5-6)

B. God is angered and hurt when people sin.

1. Concerning Israel, God's people: "They provoked him to jealousy with strange gods, with abominations provoked they him to anger." (Deuteronomy 32:16)

II. GOD IDENTIFIES WITH SUFFERING:

A. God suffers with His chosen people:

1. (Text above)
2. "And the Lord said, I have surely seen the affliction of my people which are in Egypt, and have heard their cry by reason of their taskmasters; for I know their sorrows; And I am come down to deliver them out of the hand of the Egyptians, and to bring them up out of that land unto a good land and a large, unto a land flowing with milk and honey; . . ." (Exodus 3:7, 8a)
3. On another occasion when God's people had sinned, the Bible declares: "and his soul was grieved for the misery of Israel." (Judges 10:16b)
4. Again, when God's people had sinned and departed from Him: "And the LORD God of their fathers sent to them by his messengers, . . . because he had compassion on his people, and on his dwelling place: But they mocked the messengers of God, and despised his words, and misused his prophets, until the wrath of the LORD arose against his people, till there was no remedy." (2 Chronicles 36:15, 16)

III. GOD SUFFERS WITH ALL HUMANITY – EVEN THE UNGODLY:

B. The Moabites, often times arch enemies of Israel, nonetheless brought hurt to the living God: "Therefore will I howl for Moab, and I will cry out for all Moab; mine heart shall mourn for the men of Kirheres." (Jeremiah 48:31)

IV. GOD'S PLAN OF SALVATION CAUSED HIM SUFFERING:

A. God suffered in the giving of His own Son in order that we might be saved: "For God so loved the world, that he gave his only begotten Son, that whosoever believeth in him should not perish, but have everlasting life." (John 3:16)

B. God suffers because He endures the rejection of His own Son:

   1. "He that spared not his own Son, but delivered him up for us all, how shall he not with him also freely give us all things?" (Romans 8:32)
   2. Jesus said to His disciples the following words: "He that heareth you heareth me; and he that despiseth you despiseth me; and he that despiseth me despiseth him that sent me." (Luke 10:16)

V. CONCLUSION:

Just as obedient children can bring happiness and joy to their parents, just so can people obeying the living God bring joy and delight to Him. Or on the other hand, disobedient children bring grief and sorrow to their parents, even so can any person bring pain and suffering to the living God by unbelief and willful disobedience. The Bible is very clear, " . . . them that honour me I will honour, and they that despise me shall be lightly esteemed." (I Samuel 2:30b)

THE DIVINE INVITATION TO A LOST WORLD SEPARATED FROM GOD

TEXT: "Come now, and let us reason together, saith the LORD: though your sins be as scarlet, they shall be as white as snow; though they be red like crimson, they shall be as wool." (Isaiah 1:18)

I. INTRODUCTION: Surely, it is evident to everyone that we live in a wicked and sinful world. The newspapers and TV newscasts are filled with stories of the evil and wickedness of humanity. What is wrong? For those who believe the Bible to be God's eternal Word, the answer is plain and simple. Humanity is a fallen race and apart from God much sin and evil will be manifested. But there is good news; God has provided an answer to the sinfulness of humanity. Note again, the words of our text: . . .

II. GOD'S REQUIREMENT FOR LOST HUMANITY:

A. God's Word is very plain. All of humanity is LOST! God's word declares: "For all have sinned, and come short of the glory of God;" (Romans 3:23)

1. Again, God's Word declares: " . . . There is none righteous, no, not one:" (Romans 3:10b)
2. Simply stated, each and every person needs a Saviour, and that Saviour is Jesus Christ Who died for all.

B. God is always ready to receive those who come to Him in humility and confession of sin.

1. Jesus said: "Come unto me, all ye that labour and are heavy laden, and I will give you rest. Take my yoke upon you, and learn of me; for I am meek and lowly in heart: and ye shall find rest unto your souls. For

my yoke is easy, and my burden is light." (Matthew 11:28-30)

2. The sincere prayer of the Psalmist, David, is a guide for all who come to God: "Have mercy upon me, O God, according to thy lovingkindness: according unto the multitude of thy tender mercies blot out my transgressions. Wash me throughly from mine iniquity, and cleanse me from my sin. For I acknowledge my transgressions: and my sin is ever before me. Against thee, thee only, have I sinned, and done this evil in thy sight: . . . Behold, I was shapen in iniquity, and in sin did my mother conceive me . . . Purge me with hyssop, and I shall be clean: wash me, and I shall be whiter than snow. . .Hide thy face from my sins, and blot out all mine iniquities. Create in me a clean heart, O God; and renew a right spirit within me. Cast me not away from thy presence; and take not thy holy spirit from me." (Psalms 51:1-7; 9-11)

III. **GOD'S GRACIOUS PROVISION FOR THE SINS OF HUMANITY:**

A. The only solution for human sin was and is a SAVIOUR; and that SAVIOUR is Jesus Christ, God's only Son!

1. "And that he died for all, that they which live should not henceforth live unto themselves, but unto him which died for them, and rose again." II Corinthians 5:15)

2. "For he hath made him to be sin for us, who knew no sin; that we might be made the righteousness of God in him." (II Corinthians 5:21)

Hast thou not known? Hast thou not heard, that the everlasting God, the Lord, the Creator of the ends of the earth, fainteth not, neither is weary? There is no searching of his understanding.

He giveth power to the faint; and to them that have no might he increaseth strength.

Even the youths shall faint and be weary, and young man shall utterly fall;

But they that wait upon the Lord shall renew their strength; they shall mount up with wings as eagles; they shall run, and not be weary; and they shall walk, and not faint. (Isaiah 40:28-31)

08/27/06 -- Hearthstone Cottage -- Ellensburg, WA

THE FEAR OF GOD - #2

TEXT: "The fear of the LORD is the beginning of knowledge: but fools despise wisdom and instruction". . . The fear of the LORD is the beginning of wisdom: and the knowledge of the holy is understanding." (Proverbs 1:7 and 9:10)

I. INTRODUCTION: A Biblical "fear of God" --- for those who know and love Him---is never a fear causing people to run FROM God but rather just the opposite---those who truly fear God "run TO Him." The "fear of God" of which we speak is a sense of "awe", of "reverence", and finally to those who trust and obey God, there is "love FOR God". The reality is that the vast majority of people today really DO NOT fear God! In this 21st century, we live in a world very much like that of the Apostle Paul's day, when he wrote---of the Gentile world of his day, near 2000 years ago---"There is no fear of God before their eyes." (Romans 3:18) One wonders what Paul would say of our world today!

II. THE EFFECTS OF A TRUE BIBLICAL FEAR OF GOD:

A. "The fear of the LORD is to hate evil: pride, and arrogancy, and the evil way, and the froward [perverse] mouth, do I hate." (Proverbs 8:13)

1. "Ye that love the Lord, hate evil:" (Psalm 97:10a)
2. The prophet Amos commanded, "Hate the evil, and love the good, . . . " (Amos 5:15a)

3. Of our Lord and Savior, Jesus Christ, the Bible declares, "Thou hast loved righteousness, and hated iniquity; therefore God, even thy God, hath anointed thee with the oil of gladness above thy fellows." (Hebrews 1:9)
4. "The fear of the LORD is a fountain of life, to depart from the snares of death." (Proverbs 14:27)
5. "Be not wise in thine own eyes: fear the LORD, and depart from evil." (Proverbs 3:7)
6. On the occasion of God giving the Ten Commandments to Moses, the Bible records: "And Moses said unto the people, Fear not: for God is come to prove you, and that his fear may be before your faces, that ye sin not." (Exodus 20:20)

B. The Divine response to those who truly "fear" God: "The LORD taketh pleasure in them that fear him, in those that hope in his mercy." (Psalms 147:11)

1. "The fear of the Lord tendeth to life: and he that hath it shall abide satisfied; he shall not be visited with evil." (Proverbs 19:23)
2. "The secret of the Lord is with them that fear him; and he will show them his covenant." (Psalms 25:14)
3. "Let all the earth fear the Lord: let all the inhabitants of the world stand in awe of him." (Psalms 33:8)
4. "The angel of the Lord encampeth round about them that fear him, and delivereth them." (Psalms 34:7)
5. "Like as a father pitieth (has compassion on) his children, so the Lord pitieth (has compassion on) them that fear him. For he knoweth our frame; he remembereth that we are dust." (Psalms 103:13, 14)

III. <u>CONCLUSION</u>: It was King Solomon who wrote: "Let us hear the conclusion of the whole matter: Fear God, and keep his commandments: for this is the whole duty of man." (Eccles. 12:13)

The glory of the Lord shall endure for ever: the Lord shall rejoice in his works.

He looketh on the earth, and it trembleth: he toucheth the hills, and they smoke.

I will sing unto the Lord as long as I live: I will sing praise to my God while I have my being.

My meditation of him shall be sweet: I will be glad in the Lord. (Psalm 104:31-34)

09/24/06 - Hearthstone Cottage

THE SHEPHERD PSALM

TEXT: Psalms 23:1-6

INTRODUCTION: This Psalm is a favorite of many; no doubt many people memorized it as a child. These words bring comfort and assurance especially in times of trouble, heartache, and disappointment. However, these words can be very real whatever our situation.

I. "The Lord is my shepherd . . ."

    A. Make it personal, for the "Good Shepherd, Jesus Christ" longs to have a personal relationship with each one of His sheep.

        1. "The Lord is MY Shepherd." (Emphasize the personal pronoun, "MY", as well as those throughout the entire Psalm.)

        2. Jesus declared, "I am the good shepherd: the good shepherd giveth his life for the sheep." and "I am the good shepherd, and know my sheep, and am known of mine." (John 10:11, 14).

        3. "I shall not want"

            (a) "Casting all your care upon him; for he careth for you." (I Peter 5:7)

B. "He maketh me to lie down in green pastures: he leadeth me beside the still waters. He restoreth my soul: he leadeth me in the paths of righteousness for his names' sake." (Psalms: 23:2-3)

1. "Be careful (anxious, fretful) for nothing; but in everything by prayer and supplication with thanksgiving let your requests be made known unto God." (Phil. 4:6)
2. Jesus said: "Come unto me, all ye that labour and are heavy laden, and I will give you rest." (Matthew 11:28)

II. The GOOD SHEPHERD, is not only our PROVIDER, but also our PROTECTOR:

A. "Yea, though I walk through the valley of the shadow of death, I will fear no evil: for thou art with me; thy rod and thy staff they comfort me." (Psalms 23:4)

1. To those who know, love and follow the Good Shepherd, Jesus said: " . . . lo, I am with you alway, even unto the end of the world." (Matthew 28:20b)
2. Again, " . . . for he hath said, I will never leave thee, nor forsake thee." (Hebrews 13:5b)
3. "My son, despise not thou the chastening of the Lord, nor faint when thou art rebuked of him: For whom the Lord loveth, he chasteneth. . . " (Hebrews 12:5b, 6a)

III. A MULTITUDE OF BLESSINGS FROM THE GOOD SHEPHERD:

A. "Thou preparest a table before me in the presence of mine enemies: thou anointest my head with oil; my cup runneth over. Surely goodness and mercy shall follow me all the days of my life: and I will dwell in the house of the Lord forever." (Psalms 23:5, 6)

IV. <u>CONCLUSION</u>: Again, note the personal pronouns throughout this entire Psalm; both concerning the Good Shepherd and ourselves. Relationship with the Good Shepherd, Jesus Christ is a very personal matter and is available to "whosoever will."

Oh give thanks unto the Lord; call upon his name: make known his deeds among the people.

Sing unto him, sing psalms unto him: Talk ye of all his wondrous works.

Glory ye in his holy name: let the heart of them rejoice that seek the Lord.

Seek the Lord, and his strength: seek his face evermore.

Remember his marvelous works that he hath done; his wonders, and the judgments of his mouth; (Psalm 105:1-5)

10/22/06 – 3:30 PM - Hearthstone Cottage

DESCRIPTIVE WORDS FOR THE LVIING GOD

TEXT: Psalms 18:1, 2

"I will love thee, O Lord, **my strength**. The Lord is **my rock**, and **my fortress**, and **my deliverer**; **my God**, **my strength**, in whom I will trust; **my buckler**, and **the horn of my salvation**, and **my high tower**."

<u>INTRODUCTION:</u> Note the close personal relationship with the living God, indicated by the personal pronoun**, MY** God intends for our relationship with Him to be very personal, simply because God is a personal God. Moreover, Jesus Christ died for every person and the Gospel invitation is always. . . **whosoever.**

II. THE LORD IS:

A. My. . .

1. "rock" - indicates safety and security in God's infinite and immovable strength.

"He is the Rock, his work is perfect: for all his ways are judgment: a God of truth and without iniquity, just and right is he." (Deut. 32:4)

"But the Lord is my defense; and my God is the rock of my refuge." (Psa. 94:22)

"From the end of the earth will I cry unto thee, when my heart is overwhelmed: lead me to the rock that is higher than I." (Psalms 61:2)

"He only is my rock and my salvation; he is my defence; I shall not be greatly moved." (Psalms 62:2)

> 2. "fortress" - a place of refuge and safety where the enemy cannot penetrate.
> 3. "deliverer" - a **living** protector.
> 4. "GOD," - my strength. Do we know our weakness?

Then rely on His strength!

"As for God, his way is perfect: the word of the Lord is tried: he is a buckler to all those that trust in him." (Psalms 18:30)

> 5. "buckler" - a buckler is a type of shield, symbolizing that God comes between us and harm.
> 6. "horn of my salvation" - strength and victorious power to deliver and save us.
> 7. "high tower" - a safe place to lift us above the dangers of life.

II. THE LORD or GOD IS:

> A. "My shepherd . . ." (Psalms 23:1-6)
> B. "My light and my salvation . . ." (Palms 27:1
> C. "strength and my shield . . ." (Psalms 28:7)
> D. "nigh unto them that are of a broken heart; and saveth such as be of a contrite spirit." (Psalms 34:18)
> E. "our refuge and strength, a very present help in trouble." (Psalms 46:1)

"The Lord of hosts is with us; the God of Jacob is our refuge." (Psalms 46:7

"The Lord of hosts is with us; the God of Jacob is our refuge." (Psalms 46:11)

> F. "a sun and shield: the Lord will give grace and glory: no good thing will he withhold from them that walk uprightly." (Psalms 84:11)

WORD PICTURES OF THE LIVING GOD

TEXT: "He is the Rock, his work is perfect: for all his ways are judgment: a God of truth and without iniquity, just and right is he." (Deuteronomy 32:4)

INTRODUCTION: The Holy Bible is the only reliable source of information about the living God. Within its pages we discover not only the name of God but also word pictures of who He is and what He is like. Consider the text before us:

I. "He is the Rock . . ."

    A. This word speaks of:

        1. stability. . . endurance. . .strength. . .security
        2. Illus.: The Rock of Gibralter
        3. "The Lord is my rock, and my fortress, and my deliverer; my God, my strength, in whom I will trust; . . . (Psalms 18:2a)

II. ". . .his work is perfect . . ."

    A. "Perfect" in our minds speaks of something that is flawless, without defect.

        1. Twice in the Bible, we are told that God's "way" is "perfect."

            a. "As for God, his way is perfect; the word of the Lord is tried: he is a buckler to all them that trust in him." (2 Samuel 22:31)

            b. "As for God, his way is perfect: the word of the Lord is tried: he is a buckler to all those that trust in him." (Psalms 18:30)

III. ". . .for all his ways are judgment . . .just and right is he."

    A. The word "judgment" simply means that God is "just".

        1. The living God will always do that which is "right" or "just".

            a. Perhaps the simple word "fair" which means there is no "partiality" better describes the nature and being of God. The Bible clearly states that God is "no respecter of persons."

                (1) The Apostle James tell us that the person who "respects" persons commits SIN.

        2. Simply stated: God has no favorites; i,e. He has no special "pets" who can get away with some sins while others cannot.

            a. The living God will judge on the basis of absolute truth and fairness or justice.

B. Abraham, many centuries ago asked the question: "Shall not the judge of all the earth do right?" (Genesis 18:25b)

   1. God had come to Abraham informing him of the coming judgment upon the Sodomites because of their moral filth and wickedness. Abraham was concerned about his nephew living in Sodom and questioned whether God would destroy the righteous with the wicked.

IV. ". . .a God of truth and without iniquity . . ."

   A. It was Jesus who said, "I am the way, the truth, and the life . . .:" (John 14:6a)

      1. Of Jesus, the Bible records, "For he hath made him to be sin for us, who knew no sin; that we might be made the righteousness of God in him." (2 Cor. 5:21)

THE DIVINE INVITATION TO A LOST WORLD SEPARATED FROM GOD

TEXT: "Come now, and let us reason together, saith the Lord: though your sins be as scarlet, they shall be as white as snow; though they be red like crimson, they shall be as wool." (Isaiah 1:18)

I. INTRODUCTION: Surely, it is evident to everyone that we live in a wicked and sinful world. The newspapers and TV newscasts are filled with stories of the evil and wickedness of humanity. What is wrong? For those who believe the Bible to be God's eternal Word, the answer is plain and simple. Humanity is a fallen race and apart from God much sin and evil will be manifested. But there is good news; God has provided an answer to the sinfulness of humanity. Note again, the words of our text: . . .

II. **GOD'S REQUIREMENT FOR LOST HUMANITY**:

    A. God's Word is very plain. All of humanity is LOST! God's word declares: "For all have sinned, and come short of the glory of God;" (Romans 3:23)

        1. Again, God's Word declares: " . . . There is none righteous, no, not one." (Romans 3:10b)
        2. Simply stated, each and every person needs a Saviour, and that Saviour is Jesus Christ Who died for all.

    B. God is always ready to receive those who come to Him in humility and confession of sin.

        1. Jesus said: "Come unto me, all ye that labor and are heavy laden, and I will give you rest. Take my yoke upon you, and learn of me; for I am meek and lowly in heart: and ye shall find rest unto your souls. For

my yoke is easy, and my burden is light." (Matthew 11:28-30)

2. The sincere prayer of the Psalmist, David, is a guide for all who come to God: "Have mercy upon me, O God, according to thy loving kindness: according unto the multitude of thy tender mercies blot out my transgressions. Wash me throughly from mine iniquity, and cleanse me from my sin. For I acknowledge my transgressions: and my sin is ever before me. Against thee, thee only, have I sinned, and done this evil in thy sight: . . . Behold, I was shapen in iniquity, and in sin did my mother conceive me. . . Purge me with hyssop, and I shall be clean: wash me, and I shall be whiter than snow. . . Hide thy face from my sins, and blot out all mine iniquities. Create in me a clean heart, O God; and renew a right spirit within me. Cast me not away from thy presence; and take not thy holy spirit from me." (Psalms 51: 1-5; 7, 9-11)

III. <u>GOD'S GRACIOUS PROVISION FOR THE SINS OF HUMANITY</u>:

A. The only solution for human sin was and is a SAVIOUR; and that SAVIOUR is Jesus Christ, God's only Son!

1. "And that he died for all, that they which live should not henceforth live unto themselves, but unto him which died for them, and rose again." (II Corinthians 5:15)
2. "For he hath made him to be sin for us, who knew no sin; that we might be made the righteousness of God in him." (II Corinthians 5:21)
3. Peter declared: "Who his own self bare our sins in his own body on the tree, that we, being dead to sins, should live unto righteousness: by whose stripes ye were healed." (I Peter 2:24)

B. God in love, mercy, and grace has provided salvation for all mankind; however, God will never force anyone to serve Him. God has made provision for ALL mankind, but He will never FORCE anyone to serve Him.

1. God has given every person the power of CHOICE; i.e. we all have a free will. We are free to accept God's gracious offer or we may reject it.
2. When God placed man in the beautiful Garden of Eden, Adam and Eve were free to obey God or disobey Him. Sadly, they chose to yield to temptation and disobeyed the direct commandment of God, and sin entered the human race.
3. And so it is today, each one of us is FREE to accept God's offer of eternal salvation in Jesus Christ or we are FREE to reject it and go our own way.

IV. **CONCLUSION:** Both Matthew and Luke record Jesus weeping over the city of Jerusalem: "O Jerusalem, Jerusalem, thou that killest the prophets, and stonest them which are sent unto thee, how often would I have gathered thy children together, even as a hen gathereth her chickens under her wings, and ye would not!" (Matthew 23:37)

And Again, "O Jerusalem, Jerusalem, which killest the prophets, and stonest them that are sent unto thee; how often would I have gathered thy children together, as a hen doth gather her brood under her wings, and ye would not!" (Luke 13:34)

4/22/07 – 3:30 – HEARTHSTONE COTTAGE

BELIEVE ON / IN THE
LORD JESUS CHRIST

TEXT: " . . . Sirs, what must I do to be saved? And they said, Believe on the Lord Jesus Christ, and thou shalt be saved." (Acts 16:30b, 31a)

I. **INTRODUCTION**: Briefly give the background for the question & response. The question asked by the Philippian jailer is a question of eternal consequence! It is a question every human being should ask! "What must I do to be saved?" Eternal destiny hangs in the balance. Consider how the Apostles answered this question:

II. **WHAT DOES IT MEAN TO BELIEVE?**

   A. This is a "verb" which designates action or response. Literally, it means "to be persuaded of, or to place confidence in, to trust; therefore, it means to rely upon, not mere passively accepting something as fact."

   1. To Illustrate:

      a. It is one thing to "believe" a train or plane or car will take you to a certain place----it is quite another

107

to actually get on that machine and let it take you to your destination.

b. When Peter saw Jesus walking on the water of the Sea of Galilee (Matthew 14:25-32), he questioned Jesus and said, " . . .if it be thou, bid me come unto thee on the water." Jesus simply said to Peter, "Come." "And when Peter was come down out of the ship, he walked on the water, to go to Jesus." Had Peter not put his faith and obedience into action he would never have walked on the water.

c. And so it is with "believing" in Jesus Christ. "Believing" enough to actually and personally place our faith in Jesus Christ to "save" us.

d. Please note: Paul did not tell the jailer to be (1) a good person; (2) join a church; (3) pay a certain amount of money to charity; (4) or even to keep the Ten Commandments. While all of these things may be good in their place; not one of them or all of them put together can ever save us! Our personal salvation depends upon our trusting Jesus Christ to save us; believing that His death upon the Cross is the only means of our salvation.

B. Again, note the fact that the Apostle was very clear and specific: It is Jesus Christ Who alone can save us. This is why He came. He came to give us eternal life if we would but come to Him. God has done His part; we are responsible to do our part, which is to believe in Jesus Christ enough to bring to obedience.

III. **WHAT DOES IT MEAN TO BE "SAVED?"**

A. Because of human sin, we need a Savior for we cannot save ourselves. The word "saved" speaks of "deliverance" or freedom from sin.

1. Believing in and receiving Jesus Christ our Saviour by simple faith can bring eternal salvation to all who obey the invitation of our Lord.

   a. Jesus said, "Come unto me, all ye that labour and are heavy laden, and I will give you rest." (Matthew 11:28)

   b. "Come now, and let us reason together, saith the Lord: though your sins be as scarlet, they shall be as white as snow; though they be red like crimson, they shall be as wool." (Isaiah 1:18)

   c. About 700 years before Jesus was born, the Prophet Isaiah declared: "Surely he hath borne our griefs, and carried our sorrows: yet we did esteem him stricken, smitten of God, and afflicted. But he was wounded for our transgressions, he was bruised for our iniquities: the chastisement of our peace was upon him; and with his stripes we are healed. All we like sheep have gone astray; we have turned every one to his own way; and the Lord hath laid on him the iniquity of us all." (Isaiah 53:4-6)

05/27/07 – HEARTHSTONE COTTAGE

<u>JESUS' PROMISE TO RETURN</u>

TEXT: "Let not your heart be troubled: ye believe in God, believe also in me. 2. In my Father's house are many mansions: if it were not so, I would have told you. I go to prepare a place for you. 3. And if I go and prepare a place for you, I will come again, and receive you unto myself; that where I am, there ye may be also. 4. And whither I go ye know, and the way ye know. 5. Thomas saith unto him, Lord, we know not whither thou goest; and how can we know the way? 6. Jesus saith unto him, I am the way, the truth, and the life: no man cometh unto the Father, but by me." (John 14:1-6)

I. INTRODUCTION: Jesus said these words to His disciples because of what He had just spoken to them in (John 13:36-38): "Simon Peter said unto him, Lord, whither goest thou? Jesus answered him, Whither I go, thou canst not follow me now; but thou shalt follow me afterwards. 37. Peter said unto him, Lord, why cannot I follow thee now? I will lay down my life for thy sake. 38. Jesus answered him, Wilt thou lay down thy life for my sake? Verily, verily, I say unto thee, The cock shall not crow, till thou hast denied me thrice."

II. MANY MANSIONS -- AT HOME WITH THE HEAVENLY FATHER:

A. The Apostle Paul spoke of that which God is preparing for those who love Him: "But as it is written, Eye hath not seen, nor ear heard, neither have entered into the heart of man, the things which God hath prepared for them that love him." (I Corinthians 2:9)

  1. Heaven -- It is our heavenly home with the Father and with Jesus!

      a. ". . . I go to prepare a place for you" . . . and "that where I am, there ye may be also." (John14:2b, 3b)

  2. Jesus has gone before us to prepare a place (home) for those who love Him!

      a. Again, to the Corinthian church the Apostle Paul wrote: "For we know that if our earthly house of this tabernacle were dissolved, we have a building of God, an house not made with hands, eternal in the heavens." (2 Corinthians 5:1)

III. JESUS' PROMISE TO RETURN FOR THOSE WHO LOVE HIM:

A. "I will come again . . ."

  1. Literally, it is: "And I shall take you along to my own home."

a. These words are fulfilled in death for all believers who die before Jesus comes to this earth again.

b. And REMEMBER: Jesus said, "I WILL COME AGAIN."

c. Moreover, it is heaven for the believer to be where Jesus is and to be with Him forever!

d. Song: "Where Jesus is, 'tis heaven there." To receive and know Jesus Christ as Savior and Lord NOW, in this life, is but a foretaste of eternity with our Lord!

IV. "I AM THE WAY, THE TRUTH, AND THE LIFE"

A. Jesus responds to Thomas' question, "Lord, we know not whither thou goest; and how can we know the way?" (John 14:5b)

1. To Martha in (John 11:25b) Jesus said, "I am the resurrection and the life. . ."

2. To the Pharisees, Jesus said, "I am the door." (John 10:7); and "the light of the world" (John 8:12)

3. No man / person can come unto the Father except by / through Jesus Christ!

V. CONCLUSION: The Scripture often declares, "WHOSOEVER WILL MAY COME:"

06/24/07 – HEARTHSTONE COTTAGE

THAT WHICH PLEASES THE LIVING GOD

TEXT: "Wherewith shall I come before the Lord, and bow myself before the high God? Shall I come before him with burnt offerings, with calves of a year old? (7) Will the Lord be pleased with thousands of rams, or with ten thousands of rivers of oil? Shall I give my firstborn for my transgression, the fruit of my body for the sin of my soul? (8) He hath shewed thee, O man, what is good: and what doth the Lord require of thee, but to do justly and to love mercy, and to walk humbly with thy God?" (Micah 6:6-8)

INTRODUCTION: Pleasing or honoring God ought to be a priority for all who would seek a vital relationship with God. The Scripture declares that God was pleased with His Son. At the baptism of Jesus, it is recorded: "And lo a voice from heaven, saying, This is my beloved Son, in whom I am well pleased." (Matthew 3:17)

Again, at Jesus' transfiguration, a voice came from heaven, " . . . This is my beloved Son, in whom I am well pleased;" (Matthew 17:5b)

I. QUESTION: HOW SHALL I COME BEFORE . . . OR APPROACH GOD?

    A. Shall I bring an expensive sacrifice?

        1. Many think so; i.e. that it is possible to buy Divine favor.

        2. If I just give enough money or property---something.

113

3. If I live by the "golden rule." Then God will hear me.
4. If I work hard enough in the church or do great humanitarian works.
   (a) Help feed the poor.
   (b) Help a disabled person cross the street.
5. If I am honest and pay my taxes, never cheating the city, county or government.
6. If I give my son or daughter sacrificially for mission work or the ministry.

B. In short: all of the above is simply another way of saying, "By some good deed or work, God will be obligated to bless me . . . prosper me . . . and more importantly, grant unto me eternal life."

II. CONSIDER THE DIVINE ANSWER TO THE QUESTIONS OF OUR TEXT:

A. "Do justly." Fairness, honesty---not doing right in order to gain God's favor, but because we are His children.

1. The prophet Micah was talking to "God's people". Therefore, they were to live out the spirit and heart of God in relation to others.

B. "To love mercy."

1. Kind, compassionate, considerate of the needs of others. These attributes can only come as a result of a vital relationship with God, thus being like Him.

C. "Walk humbly with thy God."

   1. That is, showing a meek and submissive spirit and attitude in our relationship with God and with others. No arrogance or pride of person here.

III. <u>CONCLUSION</u>: Note, the words of our text: To the questions asked, God gives the Divine answer ---"He hath shown thee, O man . . ." (Verse 8 is God's answer.)

07/29/07 – HEARTHSTONE COTTAGE

3:30 -- 4:00 P.M. -- Series # 1.

JESUS CHRIST -- THE GREAT 'I AM

TEXT: "Jesus said unto them, I am the bread of life: he that cometh to me shall never hunger; and he that believeth on me shall never thirst . . . I am that bread of life . . . This is that bread which came down from heaven: not as your fathers did eat manna, and are dead: he that eateth of this bread shall live forever." (John 6:35, 48, 58)

INTRODUCTION: Significantly, seven (7) times in the Gospel of John Jesus uses the simple phrase, "I am". Each one emphasizes an important aspect of the personal ministry of Jesus. The other "I am" statements are: "I am the light of the world" (8:12); "I am the door" (10:9); "I am the good shepherd" (10:11, 14); "I am the resurrection and the life" (11:25); "I am the way, the truth, and the life" (14:6); "I am the vine" (15, 5).

I. "**I AM THE BREAD OF LIFE**":

    A. Jesus takes the most common source of physical, natural human food -- "bread" – and declares, "I am the bread of life."

        1. There should not be any misunderstanding here -- obviously, He is not speaking of Himself as "physical" food, but rather of "spiritual " food and life.

2. Just as physical food can never feed us unless we eat / partake of it; just so, Jesus Christ, the spiritual bread of life cannot feed our souls, our spirit unless we partake of Him by faith.

   (a) To live physically, we have to eat physical food. And to live spiritually we must partake of Him Who is spiritual food, that is, the spiritual "bread" of life.

3. The Apostle Paul declared in his letter to the church at Colosse that, "Christ, who is our life," (Colossians 3:4)

4. Physical "hunger" and physical "thirst" are two of the most demanding needs of our human bodies. We cannot live without food and we cannot live without water.

   (a) But we must "partake" of them or they are useless to our bodies.

   (b) And it is also true that we cannot "live" spiritually apart from Him Who is "life", Jesus Christ, which also means we must receive Him as our spiritual life.

II. **HOW DO WE PARTAKE OF THIS "BREAD OF LIFE"?**

A. Jesus said in John 10:10! "I am come that they might have life, and that they might have it more abundantly." Here is the reason Jesus came into this world --- that He might give "life", that is, "eternal life" to all who would receive Him.

   1. But Jesus also said in John 5:40 -- "And ye will not come to me, that ye might have life."

2. The Divine invitation is always open to "whosoever" will respond.

   (a) Again, Jesus said: "Come unto me, all ye that labour and are heavy laden, and I will give you rest." (Matthew 11:28)

B. We come to God by faith and in obedience to His Word, for He said, "Come unto me."

  1. "But without faith it is impossible to please him; for he that cometh to God must believe that he is, and that he is a rewarder of them that diligently seek him." (Hebrews 11:6)

  2. Many times people say: "I cannot believe in anything that I cannot see." How foolish!

   (a) Have you ever seen a "germ" or "virus"? But we know what they do! Therefore, we believe and know they exist.

   (b) Has anyone ever "seen" the wind? But we can see and know what it does. We can "see" the leaves and branches of the trees move, but we cannot "see" the wind itself.

   (c) Has anyone ever seen "pain"? But we can feel it and know it or "see" its effect on ourselves or someone else suffering pain.

C. Though we cannot "see" God with our natural physical eyes, yet God has provided ample proof of His presence and existence.

  1. The Apostle Paul in writing to the Roman church said, "For the invisible things of him from the creation of the world are clearly seen, being understood by the things

that are made, even his eternal power and Godhead; so that they are without excuse:" (Romans 1:20)

2. God in His goodness and mercy has provided ample "proof" of Who and what He is, by the things (the world and all its creatures, etc.) made by Him.

   (a) Note that God's Word says,". . .**they are without excuse."**

III. CONCLUSION: God has revealed Himself in many ways, but the most important way is in the person of His Son, Jesus Christ, Who came to reveal the Father. That Jesus Christ was born, lived and died in this world cannot be refuted! His invitation is still open to "whosever" will believe His word of invitation and come to Him. And remember, Jesus said, "**Come unto me," "and him that cometh to me I will in no wise cast out."** (Mathew 11:28 & John 6:37)

08/26/07 – HEARTHSTONE COTTAGE

Ellensburg, WA 98926
3:30 - 4:00 PM -- Series # 2.

JESUS CHRIST -- THE GREAT 'I AM

TEXT: "Then spake Jesus again unto them, saying, I am the light of the world: he that followeth me shall not walk in darkness, but shall have the light of life." (John 8:12)

INTRODUCTION: Darkness can be a terrible enemy. In physical darkness we can easily walk into some unseen object or fall, stumble and injure ourselves. Light, on the other hand, exposes or reveals that which may cause personal harm--allowing us to prevent serious injury. Likewise, in the spiritual realm we desperately need light to guide us in order to prevent eternal spiritual harm and loss. JESUS CHRIST is that LIGHT we all desperately need, for Jesus said, "I AM THE LIGHT OF THE WORLD."

I. **I AM**": Consider the times Jesus said, "I AM" -- (Seven times in John's gospel): "I am the bread of life," (considered last month); (today) "I am the light of the world;" then "I am the door;" again, "I am the good shepherd;" and again, "I am the resurrection and the life;" and then, "I am the way, the truth, and the life;" and finally, "I am the true vine."

II. <u>"I AM THE LIGHT OF THE WORLD"</u>:

A. Light is of no value unless we are willing to personally use that light.

1. Obviously, Jesus here was talking about spiritual light, not the light of the moon or the sun or any artificial light.
2. Tragically, many people would rather walk in the darkness of sin and disobedience to God, rather than walk in God's light.

   a. Jesus said, "And this is the condemnation, that light is come into the world, and men loved darkness rather than light, because their deeds were evil. . . A simple knowledge of the whole Bible, but what we contend is this: that taking a line at a time, verse at a time, or truth at a time, it cannot be hard to understand. One cannot look at any big book and get all of its contents at a glance. A man is foolish to say the Bible is hard to understand. He that doeth evil hateth the light, neither cometh to the light, lest his deeds should be reproved. But he that doeth truth cometh to the light, that his deeds may be made manifest, that they are wrought in God." (John 3:19-21)

III. <u>"HE THAT FOLLOWETH ME SHALL NOT WALK IN DARKNESS</u>. . .:

A. Jesus often invited people by simply saying, "follow me."

1. His invitation is so simple, so direct, that no one need misunderstand it.
    a. Notice: "FOLLOW ME," that is, "come to me, trust me, believe and obey my word and be willing to be my disciple.

B. Note the result:

1. We will no longer walk in darkness, but rather, we shall have the light of life.

    a. That is, we will have the "good shepherd" as our friend and guide.
    b. Remember, Jesus said, "I am the light of the world."

        (1) An old song exhorts: "Turn your eyes upon Jesus."

C. We can only have light---if we are willing to follow that light; that is, be followers of Jesus Christ

III. JESUS SAID, "COME UNTO ME"; HIS INVITATION IS STILL OPEN:

9/23/07 – HEARTHSTONE COTTAGE

Ellensburg, WA 98926
3:30 - 4:00 -- Series # 3

JESUS CHRIST -- THE DOOR

TEXT: "I am the door: by me if any man enter in, he shall be saved, and shall go in and out, and find pasture." (John 10:7 and 9)

INTRODUCTION: Jesus often used the words, "I Am". We have considered His words in John 6:35, 48, and 51, where He stated "I Am the bread of life"; then also, His words in John 8:12, "I Am the light of the world." Today we consider His words "I Am the door." Jesus used various words to make clear the truth that He is the One who alone can satisfy our every spiritual need.

I. "I AM THE DOOR:"

A. The purpose of a door is obvious -- it is either a means of entrance or exit.

1. Jesus here spoke of entrance, for He said: ". . . .by me if any man enter in, he shall be save. . ."
2. Perhaps we have all heard the old saying, "All roads lead to Rome."
3. From the words Jesus said, we must conclude that NOT all roads lead to eternal life.

        (a) For He said, ". . . .by me if any man enter in, he shall be saved. . ."

    B. The way to God is through Jesus Christ and no other, for in John 14:6, Jesus said, " . . .no man cometh unto the Father, but by me."

        1. No wonder the Apostle Paul declared, "For I determined not to know anything among you, save Jesus Christ, and him crucified." (I Corinthians 2:2)

           (a) The message Paul preached was -- Jesus Christ! Likewise the Apostle Peter declared before the Jewish Council, "Neither is there salvation in any other; for there is none other name under heaven given among men, whereby we must be saved." (Acts 4:12)

II. THE DOOR -- JESUS CHRIST -- ENTRANCE TO LIFE AND A LIVING RELATIONSHIP WITH THE LIVING GOD:

    A. While Jesus Christ is the door or entrance to salvation or eternal life; He is also the door to a living relationship to God

        1. Hymn: "In The Garden"

           (a) The Chorus states: "And He walks with me and He talks with me . . ."

        2. A person does not become saved and then stand-alone -- God means for us to continue to draw our very spiritual life from Him who is LIFE!!

III. CONCLUSION: He who is THE DOOR, also said, "Come unto me . . . " Tragically, He had to say to some, "Bui you will not come to me . . ." But the invitation is still open, "COME UNTO ME"

10/28/07 – HEARTHSTONE COTTAGE

Ellensburg, WA 98926
3:30 - 4:00 P.M. -- Series # 4

JESUS CHRIST – THE GREAT "I AM"

I. **INTRODUCTION:** We have considered thus far the words of Jesus in John's Gospel declaring who He was / is: Jesus said, "I am the bread of life," "I am the light of the world," then last time, "I am the door." Today I want to consider with you Jesus' words, "I am the good shepherd: the good shepherd giveth his life for the sheep." . . . "I am the good shepherd, and know my sheep, and am known of mine." (John 10:11 and 14)

II. **I AM THE GOOD SHEPHERD:** "I am the good shepherd: the good shepherd giveth his life for the sheep." (John 10:11) No one else the good shepherd---only JESUS CHRIST!

   A. Jesus Christ, the good shepherd; the word "shepherd" carries great meaning. . .

      1. The "good shepherd" **cares** for His sheep.

         (a) Peter declares our privilege: "Casting all your care upon him, for he careth for you."
         (b) Contrast Peter's declaration with how the Psalmist must have felt when in great need: "I looked on my right hand, and beheld, but there was no man

126

that would know me: refuge failed me; **no man cared for my soul**." (Psalms 142:4)

(c) Again, Jesus said: "Come unto me, all ye that labour and are heavy laden, and I will give you rest." (Matthew 11:28)

2. Tragically, too few come to Jesus Christ, even though an invitation has been given.

(a) Jesus said: "And ye will not come to me, that ye might have life." (John 5:40)

(b) Again, Jesus said: "Behold, I stand at the door, and knock: if any man hear my voice, and open the door, I will come in to him, and will sup with him, and he with me." (Revelation 3:20)

III. "THE GOOD SHEPHERD GIVETH HIS LIFE FOR THE SHEEP:"

A. Jesus came to seek and save the lost

1. Jesus gave the parable or story of the man with 100 sheep; however, one was lost and no longer in the fold. The shepherd searched until he found his lost sheep.

(a) "I say unto you, that likewise joy shall be in heaven over one sinner that repenteth, more than over ninety and nine just persons, which need no repentance." (Luke 15:7)

B. In order for the sheep to be saved, the shepherd had to give himself---thus providing salvation and life for the sheep.

1. John 10:11b -- "the good shepherd giveth his life for the sheep."

  (a) In order for anyone, any person to have eternal life, a sacrifice had to be made to purchase that eternal life. JESUS CHRIST IS THAT SACRIFICE!

 2. The Apostle Peter declared: "Neither is there salvation in any other; for there is none other name under heaven given among men, whereby we must be saved." (Acts 4:12)

IV. "I . . . KNOW MY SHEEP AND AM KNOWN OF MINE." (John 10:14)

 A. Jesus knows those who are His sheep and those sheep know Him as their Lord and Savior, their personal "good shepherd."

 B. Thus each person needs to ask: DO I KNOW THE GOOD SHEPHERD?

I will bless the Lord at all times: his praise shall continually be in my mouth.

My soul shall make her boast in the Lord: the humble shall hear thereof, and be glad.

O magnify the Lord with me, and let us exalt his name together.

I sought the Lord, and he heard me, and delivered me from all my fears.

They looked unto him, and we're lightened: and their faces were not ashamed.

This poor man cried, and the Lord heard him, and saved him out of all his troubles.

The angel of the Lord encampeth round about them that fear him, and delivereth them.

O taste and see that the Lord is good: blessed is the man that trusteth in him.

O fear the Lord, you his saints: for there is no want to them that fear him. (Psalms 34:1-9)

12/30/07 – HEARTHSTONE COTTAGE

Ellensburg, WA 98926
3:30 - 4:00 P.M. -- Series # 5.

JESUS CHRIST -- I AM THE RESURRECTION AND THE LIFE

TEXT: "Jesus said unto her, (Martha) I am the resurrection, and the life: he that believeth in me, though he were dead, yet shall he live: And whosoever liveth and believeth in me shall never die. Believest thou this?" (John 11:25, 26)

I. **INTRODUCTION**: Thus far in this series we have considered the following statements of Jesus concerning Himself. Each statement emphasizes an important aspect of the personal ministry of Jesus: 1) "I am the bread of life" (John 6:35, 48, 58); "I am the light of the world" (John 8:12); "I am the door" (John 10:9); "I am the good shepherd" (John 10:11, 14); {today}, "I am the resurrection, and the life" (John 11:25, 26); "I am the way, the truth, and the life:" (John 14:6); and finally, "I am the vine" (John 15: 4-5).

II. **WORDS OF COMFORT IN THE TIME OF SORROW**:

A. The separating of loving human relationships is never easy! Therefore, Jesus, in love and compassion, sought to turn Mary and Martha's attention to the reality of a coming resurrection and eternal life.

1. Jesus said: "And whosoever liveth and believeth in me shall never die."
2. In John 14:1-6 Jesus makes very clear that there is a life after death, that the life in this world is not the end of existence.

   (a) Jesus said, "I go to prepare a place for you." (John 14:2b)
   (b) This is the "blessed" and "glorious" promise to all believers.

III. **"WHOSOEVER LIVETH AND BELIEVETH IN ME SHALL NEVER DIE**

A. Consider the word "whosoever":

1. The door is still open to "whosoever".
2. Forgiveness of sin, peace, a vital relationship with the living God, yet today, is God's gracious promise to "whosoever" will receive His gift.

B. The qualifications or requirements for receiving these gifts and blessings are very simple:

1. We must "believe" the Gospel -- notice what Jesus said to Martha: "Believest thou this?"

   (a) Note Martha's response: "Yea, Lord, I believe that thou art the Christ, the Son of God, which should come into the world."
   (b) John 3:16 -- Believing faith or trust requires "action", i.e. do we "believe" enough to "call" upon the Savior and by faith receive Him?

C. "Believe" and then "live" for the Saviour and Redeemer, Jesus Christ!

D. Consider the promise of Jesus quoted earlier in this message:

(a) "I go to prepare a place for you." And then the words, "I will come again, and receive you unto myself; that where I am, there ye may be also." (John 14:3b)

IV. <u>CONCLUSION</u>: <u>WHAT WILL "YOU" DO WITH JESUS?</u>

A. Relationship with the living God is an individual, personal relationship.

1. Jesus said, "Come unto me . . ."
2. Some of the last words of Jesus in Revelation 3:20 declare: "Behold, I stand at the door, and knock: if any man hear my voice, and open the door, I will come in to him, and will sup with him, and he with me." Relationship with Jesus "now" and "for eternity" as we remain faithful to Him! This is His promise to "WHOSOEVER."

01/27/08 – HEARTHSTONE COTTAGE

Ellensburg, WA 98926
3:30 -- 4:00 PM (Series # 6)

I AM THE WAY, THE TRUTH, AND THE LIFE

TEXT: (1) "Let not your heart be troubled: ye believe in God, believe also in me. (2) In my Father's house are many mansions: if it were not so, I would have told you. I go to prepare a place for you. (3) And if I go and prepare a place for you, I will come again, and receive you unto myself; that where I am, there ye may be also. (4) And whither I go ye know, and the way ye know. (5) Thomas saith unto him, Lord, we know not whither thou goest; and how can we know the way? (6) Jesus saith unto him, I am the way, the truth, and the life: no man cometh unto the Father, but by me." (John 14:1 - 6)

INTRODUCTION: To Martha, Jesus had called Himself "the life" "I am the resurrection and the life:" (11:25); to the Pharisees Jesus had declared Himself to be "the door" (10:7); and then "the light of the world" (8:12). In the text before us, Jesus is declaring He is the "way", He is the "truth", and He is the "life."

I. "I am the way."

A. There are many "ways" to arrive at the White House in Washington, DC, or we might choose any other physical destination.

1. Our conveyance may be by car, bus, train, or airplane -- and then we might take the shortest and most direct route or one that will take us indirectly.

B. However, Jesus here is saying He is "the way" to God and finally "the way" to the place He has gone to prepare for all those who will believe and follow Him!

1. Sadly, there are those that declare "there are many ways to God."

    (a) Simply join the church and be baptized.
    (b) Never lie, always tell the truth.
    (c) Work hard and be just as good as you can
    (d) Be a faithful husband / or wife.
    (e) Be honest and pay your bills, never cheat anyone.
    (f) Be a good person and obey the laws of the land.

2. All these and many more are commendable and ought to be done--but not one or all of them can give us eternal life and a home in heaven.
3. We are not saying here that "my" church or "your" church is the way to God; we are simply saying that **Jesus Christ** is the **one** and **only** way to God!

    (a) An old hymn asks the question -- "What will you do with Jesus?" This is the real issue!

II. "I am the truth."

A. Jesus Christ, the only begotten Son of God, is the perfect revelation of the living God!

1. Do we want to know what God is like? What God thinks of sin and evil? Any question we may have about God is answered in the person of Jesus Christ!

(a) In fact, Jesus Himself declared, "He that hath seen me, hath seen the Father."

(b) Note: Jesus said, "If ye had known me, ye should have known my father also: and from henceforth ye know him, and have seen him. Philip saith unto him, Lord, show us the Father, and it sufficieth us. Jesus saith unto him, Have I been so long time with you, and yet hast thou not known me, Philip? he that hath seen me hath seen the Father; and how sayest thou then, Show us the Father? (John 14:7-9)

(c) Jesus Christ is the perfect representation of God, the Father!

2. In John 10:38 Jesus declared ". . . the Father is in me, and I in him."

(a) The Apostle Paul declared, "In hope of eternal life, which God that cannot lie, promised before the world began." (Titus 1:2)

III. "I am the life."

A. There is "physical life" and there is "spiritual" life.

1. The Bible declares, "And the Lord God formed man of the dust of the ground, and breathed into his nostrils the breath of life; and man became a living soul." (Genesis 2:7)

2. Note the two realities -- man made (physically) of the dust of the ground, and then (spiritually), from the very life breath of God, man became a living soul.

3. In John 10:27, 28 -- Jesus said, "My sheep hear my voice, and I know them, and they follow me: And I give unto them eternal life, and they shall never perish, . . ."

B. Note the last part of Jesus' words in our text: ". . .no man cometh unto the Father, but by me." (John 14:6b)

   1. Jesus Christ is not only "the bread of life," and "the light of the world," and "the door," and "the good shepherd," and "the resurrection and the life," but He also is "LIFE" in the greatest sense of the word! JEUS CHRIST IS OUR LIFE!

C. No wonder the Apostle Paul declared to the Corinthian church (I Cor. 2:2) "For I determined not to know anything among you, save Jesus Christ, and him crucified."

IV. <u>CONCLUSION</u>: Do you truly want to know abundant life? Jesus said, "I am come that they might have life, and that they might have it more abundantly." (John 10:10b)

There is ONE Saviour and one ONLY -- and His name is JESUS CHRIST!

Jesus came to deal with the problem of human sin and thus for those who will receive Him, He longs to give the gift of eternal life! Consider again the words of Jesus Christ who said, ". . .and him that cometh to me I will in no wise cast out." (John 6:37b)

2/24/08 - HEARTHSTONE COTTAGE

Ellensburg, WA 98926-3917
3:30 -- 4:00 P.M. (Series # 7)

I AM THE TRUE VINE

I. **INTRODUCTION**: We have considered in this series the Biblical statements by Jesus Christ concerning Himself and His ministry. Thus far we have considered: (1) "I am the bread of life" {John 6:35, 48, 58}; (2) "I am the light of the world" {John 8:12}; (3) "I am the door" {John 10:9}; (4) "I am the good shepherd" {"John 10:11, 14}; (5) "I am the resurrection and the life" {John 11:25, 256}; (6) "I am the way, the truth, and the life" {John 14:6} and today; (7) "**I am the vine**." {John 15:5}.

II. "**I AM THE VINE, YE ARE THE BRANCHES**": (Verse 4)

   A. Note the words of Jesus in (John 15: 4) "Abide in me, and I in you. As the branch cannot bear fruit of itself, except it abide in the vine; no more can ye, except ye abide in me."

      1. Apply these words in a natural setting and we understand it. But Jesus is using an easily understood physical or earthly reality to emphasize a spiritual truth. Obviously, fruit cannot be produced by a dead branch.

(a) Life exists only in the vine and that life flows to all the branches so long as they are joined to the vine.

(b) Applied spiritually, we have spiritual life only as we are joined to the vine---and Jesus Christ is that spiritual vine. Apart from Jesus Christ there is no spiritual life!

The Apostle Paul in writing to the New Testament church in Colossians declared that". . . Christ, who is our life, . . ." (Colossians 3:4). Apart from a personal relationship with Jesus Christ we have no spiritual life. Jesus had already said in (John 14:6b) "I am the way, the truth, and the life: no man cometh unto the Father, but by me."

B. Again, in (John 5:40) Jesus rebuked his listeners when He said, "And ye will not come to me, that ye might have life."

1. Moreover, Jesus declared in (John 10:10): "I am come that they might have life, and that they might have it more abundantly."

(a) We would think a person in desperate need physically, emotionally or mentally most foolish if he refused help that was being offered to him.

(b) No person has the ability to "**save himself**". If we could "**save ourselves**" there would have been no need for Jesus to die on the cross for our sins!

2. Consider again the words of Jesus in (John 10:11): "I am the good shepherd: the good shepherd giveth his life for the sheep."

III. <u>A LIVING RELATIONSHJIP WITH JESUS CHRIST PRODUCES REAL FRUIT:</u>

A. Jesus spoke about branches joined to Him bearing fruit and the Apostle Paul spoke about "the fruit of the Spirit."

1. "But the fruit of the Spirit is love, joy, peace, longsuffering, gentleness, goodness, faith, meekness, temperance: against such there is no law." (Galatians 5:22, 23)
2. An old hymn says it so eloquently: "Nothing but leaves for the Master."

IV. <u>CONCLUSION</u>: Some questions we need to ask ourselves: (1) Is Jesus Christ **my** own personal Savior? Is He **my** spiritual life? (2) Does Jesus Christ live in **my** heart and life by faith in Him alone? (3) Is **my** personal hope built on nothing less than "Jesus' blood and righteousness"? (4) Am **I** bearing spiritual fruit for his glory? (5) Do **I** really love Him?

3/30/08 – HEARTHSTONE COTTAGE

Ellensburg, WA 98926-3917
3:30--4:00 PM

EXALT (LIFT UP) THE NAME OF OUR GOD, FOR HE IS WORTHY

TEXT: "Thou art my God, and I will praise thee: thou art my God, I will exalt thee." (Psalms 118:28) cf. (Isaiah 40:12-31)

INTRODUCTION: This passage from the Book of the prophet Isaiah is one of the greatest descriptions of God in the Bible. Consider:

I. PROPHETIC QUESTIONS AND THEN ANSWERS: (Vs. 12-31)

    A. Verses 12-17 speak of God's

        1. Power (v. 12)
        2. Knowledge and understanding (vs. 13, 14)
        3. Exalted position of authority (vs. 15-17)

    B. (Vs. 18 - 31) A series of questions followed by the Divine answer

        1. The folly of idols and idol worshippers (vs. 18-20)
        2. (vs. 21) is an introduction to our incomparable living God!

3. (vs. 22-24) include statements as to God's exalted position and authority over all the earth.

4. (vs. 25-28) include further questions as to God's authority and power.

5. (vs. 29-31) declare God's ability to help and give strength to those who rely upon Him.

III. **CONCLUSION:** The Bible declares in John 1:3, "All things were made by him; and without Him was not anything made that was made." Yet, this same all-powerful and eternal living God invites all . . . everyone . . . "Come unto me, all ye that labor and are heavy laden, and I will give you rest." (Matthew 11:28)

Isaiah 40:12-31,

"Who hath measured the waters in the hollow of his hand, and meted out heaven with the span, and comprehended the dust of the earth in a measure, and weighed the mountains in scales, and the hills in a balance?

Who hath directed the Spirit of the Lord, or being his counsellor hath taught him?

With whom took he council, and who instructed him, and taught him in the path of judgment, and taught him knowledge, and shewed him the way of understanding?

Behold, the nations are as a drop of a bucket, and are counted as a small dust of the balance: behold, he taketh it up the isles as a very little thing.

And Lebanon is not sufficient to burn, nor the beasts thereof sufficient for a burnt offering.

All nations before him are as nothing; and they are counted to him less than nothing, and vanity.

To whom then will ye liken God? or what likeness will you compare unto him?

The workmen melted a graven image, and the Goldsmith spreadeth it over with gold, and casteth silver chains.

He that is so impoverished that he hath no oblation chooseth a tree that will not rot; he seeketh unto him a cunning workman to prepare a graven image, that shall not be moved.

Have ye not known? have ye not heard? hath it not been told you from the beginning? have ye not understood from the foundations of the earth?

It is he that sitteth upon the circle of the earth, and the inhabitants thereof are as grasshoppers; that stretcheth out the heavens as a curtain, and spreadeth them out as a tent to dwell in:

That bringeth the princess to nothing; he maketh the judges of the earth as vanity.

Yea, they shall not be planted; yea, they shall not be sown: yea, their stock shall not take root in the earth: and he shall also blow upon them, and they shall wither, and the whirlwind shall take them away as stubble.

To whom then will ye liken me, or shall I be equal? saith the holy one.

Lift up your eyes on high, and behold who hath created these things, that bringeth out their hosts by number: he calleth them all by names by the greatness of his might, for that he is strong in power; not one faileth.

Why sayest thou, O Jacob, and speakest, O Israel, My way is hid from the Lord, and my judgment is passed over from my God?

Hast thou not known? hast thou not heard, that the everlasting God, the Lord, the Creator of the ends of the earth, fainteth not, neither is weary? there is no searching of his understanding.

He giveth power to the faint; and to them hath no might he increaseth strength.

Even the youths shall faint and be weary, and the young men shall utterly fall:

But they that wait upon the Lord shall renew their strength; they shall mount up with wings as eagles; they shall run, and not be weary; and they shall walk, and not faint."

"My meditation of him shall be sweet: I will be glad in the Lord." (Psalms 104:34)

What a strange word in these times of hurry. Someone has summed it up as - "Hurry, Worry, and Bury." The unsaved dare not stop their activity or be alone - or they have the "blues." And often times the meditation of the wicked is only to more sin.

But meditation seems to be a lost art even among Christians. They read their Bibles, yes, but no time is given for meditation. Satan can thus keep them weak.

DIVINE GRIEF & PAIN

TEXT: "And they that escape of you shall remember me among the nations whither they shall be carried captives, **because I am broken with their whorish heart**, which hath departed from me, and with their eyes, which go awhoring after their idols: and they shall loathe themselves for the evils which they have committed in all their abominations." (Ezekiel 6:9)

I. **INTRODUCTION**: As finite human beings, we sometimes have difficulty understanding that an infinite, all-powerful, eternal God could experience the same emotions that we humans have. But we need to understand that God made man in His image; that is, we are like Him in the ability to think, to understand, to reason, we do have emotions, (to love or to hate, to suffer grief and pain be joyful or sorrowful), we have memory and many other faculties. We are un-like Him in that we do not have all power, we do not have all wisdom, we do not possess understanding in all things. We are limited, He is not, except that He will not, cannot do evil or anything wrong! God is perfect in every aspect, we are not and we desperately need Him. Consider now some of the emotions or feelings God has in relation to His creation.

II. <u>THE DIVINE GRIEF OF GOD</u>:

A. "And God saw that the wickedness of man was great in the earth, and that every imagination of the thoughts of his heart was only evil continually. And it **repented (or grieved)** the Lord that he had made man on the earth, and it grieved him at his heart." (Genesis 6:5-6)

1. The emotion or sense of "grief" and "pain" was manifest in the heart of God.
2. Man (God's creation) had sinned and God was deeply pained.
3. We need never think for a moment that God is happy or thrilled with delight when mankind disobeys and lives contrary to the Divine will.

B. "And the children of Israel said unto the Lord, We have sinned: do thou unto us whatsoever seemeth good unto thee; deliver us only, we pray thee, this day. And they put away the strange gods from among them, and served the Lord: and his soul was **grieved** for the misery of Israel." (Judges 10:15, 16)

1. Again, note the pain of God because of man's sin

C. "Forty years long was I **grieved** with this generation, and said, It is a people that do err in their heart, and they have not known my ways:" (Psalms 95:10)

1. The Divine patience and love of God was tested by the sins of His people.

D. From the prophet Isaiah: "Hear ye now, O house of David; Is it a small thing for you to weary men, but will ye **weary** my God also?" (Isaiah 7:13b)

145

1. Again, the thought is to test and try the patience and love of God.

E. "But thou hast not called upon me, O Jacob; but thou hast been **weary** of me, O Israel. . . thou hast **wearied** me with thine iniquities." (Isaiah 43:22, 24b)

   1. The words, translated "weary" and "wearied" are the same Hebrew word and simply means that it was a distress to God.

F. Return to our text from the Prophet Ezekiel: ". . . **I am broken with their whorish heart. . . "**

   1. **The word simply means God was pained and crushed by the sinfulness of His people.**

G. Consider the words in the New Testament: (Jesus)

   1. "And when he had looked round about on them with anger, being **grieved** for the hardness of their hearts, he saith unto the man, Stretch forth thine hand. And he stretched it out: and his hand was restored whole as the other." (Mark 3:5)
   2. The Apostle Paul: "And **grieve** not the Holy Spirit of God, whereby ye are sealed unto the day of redemption." (Ephesians 4:30)

      (a) The word translated grieve here means to **distress** or make **sad**.

CONCLUSION: Rather than cause God grief and pain and distress, how much better to bring Him joy and delight! Pleasing God comes from seeking to do His will and be obedient to His Word.

HEARTHSTONE COTTAGE

Ellensburg, WA 98926-34917
January 23, 2011

MARVELOUS PROMISES
FROM GOD'S WORD

TEXT: "Thy word is a lamp unto my feet, and a light unto my path." (Psalms 119:105)

INTRODUCTION: When walking or driving in dense darkness, we need a light to guide us, thus preventing an accident. Spiritually, that is what God's Word is to everyone who will trust in and obey the Word of God.

II. GOD'S MARVELOUS PROMISES:

A. "Come unto me, all ye that labour and are heavy laden, and I will give your rest." (Matthew 11:28)

   1. "Cast thy burden upon the Lord, and he shall sustain thee: he shall never suffer the righteous to be moved." (Psalms 55:22)
   2. "Commit thy way unto the Lord; trust also in him; and he shall bring it to pass." (Psalms 37:5)

3. "Draw nigh to God, and he will draw nigh to you. . . Humble yourselves in the sight of the Lord, and he shall lift you up." (James 4:8 & 10).

NOTE: In all of these promises God always gives us something to do: [We must come, we must cast, we must commit, we must draw close to God and we must humble ourselves.]

1. To the Philippian jailer, the Apostles exhorted: "Believe on the Lord Jesus Christ, and thou shalt be saved." (Acts 16:31)
2. "Trust in the Lord with all thine heart; and lean not unto thine own understanding. In all thy ways acknowledge him, and he shall direct thy paths." (Proverbs 3:5-6)
3. "Hast thou not known? hast thou not heard, that the everlasting God, the Lord, the Creator of the ends of the earth, fainteth not, neither is weary? there is no searching of his understanding. He giveth power to the faint; and to them that have no might he increaseth strength. Even thy youths shall faint and be weary, and the young men shall utterly fall; But they that wait upon the Lord shall renew their strength; they shall mount up with wings as eagles; they shall run, and not be weary; and they shall walk, and not faint." (Isaiah 40:28-31)

HEARTHSTONE COTTAGE

Ellensburg, WA 98926-3917
November 23, 2008 -- 3:30 -- 4:00 PM

REMEMBERING GOD'S BLESSINGS

<u>TEXT</u>: Psalms 103:1-5; especially vs. 3-5
"Who forgiveth all thine iniquities;
Who healeth all thy diseases;
Who redeemeth thy life from destruction;
Who crowneth thee with lovingkindness and tender mercies;
Who satisfieth thy mouth with good things; so that thy youth is renewed like the eagle's."

I. "<u>WHO FORGIVETH ALL THINE INIQUITIES</u>" (v. 3a)

 A. Every person, every human being needs Divine forgiveness of sins! None excluded!

  1. "For all have sinned, and come short of the glory of God;" (Romans 3:23)
  2. "The fool hath said in his heart, There is no God. They are corrupt, they have done abominable works, there is none that doeth good.
  3. The Lord looked down from heaven upon the children of men, to see if there were any that did understand, and seek God.

4. They are all gone aside, they are all together become filthy: there is none that doeth good, no, not one." (Psalms 14:1-3)

5. Again the inspired Psalmist declared: "If thou, Lord, shouldest mark iniquities, O Lord, who shall stand? But there is forgiveness with thee, that thou mayest be feared." (Psalms 130:3, 4)

II. **"WHO HEALETH ALL THY DISEASES"** (V. 3b)

A. "But he was wounded for our transgressions, he was bruised for our iniquities: the chastisement of our peace was upon him; and with his stripes we are healed." (Isaiah 53:5)

1. There is still physical healing through faith in Jesus Christ.

2. The worst disease of all is, SIN! And through confession, repentance and faith in Jesus Christ, the GREATEST disease of all---SIN---CAN BE CLEANSED and FORGIVEN!

    (a) Justification---"just as though we had never sinned.")

III. **"WHO REDEEMETH THY LIFE FROM DESTRUCTION"** (v. 4a)

A. SIN is a destroyer and only God through Jesus Christ can defeat it.

1. "For the wages of sin is death; but the gift of God is eternal life though Jesus Christ our Lord." (Romans 6:23)

2. "For all have sinned and come short of the glory of God;" (Romans 3:23)

IV. "WHO CROWNETH THEE WITH LOVING KINDNESS(v. 4b)

A. Notice v. 8: "The Lord is merciful and gracious, slow to anger, and plenteous in mercy."

V. "WHO SATISFIETH THY MOUTH WITH GOOD THINGS" (v. 5)

A. "Every good gift and every perfect gift is from above, and cometh down from the Father of lights, with whom is no variableness, neither shadow of turning." (James 1:17)

VI. CONCLUSION: Jesus said: "Come unto me, all ye that labor and are heavy laden, and I will give you rest. Take my yoke upon you, and learn of me; for I am meek and lowly in heart: and ye shall find rest unto your souls. For my yoke is easy, and my burden is light." (Matthew 11;28-30)

HEARTHSTONE COTTAGE

Ellensburg, WA 98926-3917
December 28, 2008 -- 3:30--4:00 PM

ETERNAL VALUES WHICH
DELIGHT THE HEART OF GOD

TEXT: "Thus saith the Lord, Let not the wise man glory in his wisdom, neither let the mighty man glory in his might, let not the rich man glory in his riches: But let him that glorieth glory in this, that he understandeth and knoweth me, that I am the Lord which exercise lovingkindness, judgment, and righteousness, in the earth: for in these things I delight, saith the Lord." (Jeremiah 9:23-24)

I. **INTRODUCTION**: Significantly, the prophet Jeremiah declares those things in which we are not to glory or exalt as virtues in our lives: wisdom, might, riches. Each one is important in its place; however, there are virtues or values more important than, more important than, any one or all of them. For God delights in values far more important than any one or all of them.

II. **"LOVINGKINDNESS"**: Dictionary def: "Affection or tenderness stemming from sincere love for someone."

   A. The Psalmist declared: "Like as a father pitieth his children, so the Lord pitieth them that fear him." (Psalms 103:13)

1. The word "pitieth" refers to love and/or compassion
2. "O Jerusalem, Jerusalem, thou that killest the prophets, and stonest them which are sent unto thee, how often would I have gathered thy children together, even as a hen gathereth her chickens under her wings, and ye would not." (Matthew 23:37)

III. **"JUDGMENT"** "judgment in the earth"

   A. Abraham asked God in Genesis 18:25b, "Shall not the judge of all the earth do right?"

      1. The obvious answer is: "Absolutely, God will always do what is right!"
      2. Not a shred of evidence will be missing when we stand in judgment before the living God. He will only and always do only that which is right, just, righteous!

IV. **"RIGHTEOUSNESS"** Simply that which is right and just morally, ethically, and spiritually.

   A. Not only is God righteous, but He requires that we live and walk in righteousness, i.e. that we do and manifest that which is right, always, by His grace and strength.

      1. With God living in our hearts and lives, we will want, desire and purpose to live in right relation to others.

V. **CONCLUSION:** Our privilege and responsibility is to live as God would have us live in every aspect of our lives. From God will come our help!

HEARTHSTONE COTTAGE

Ellensburg, WA 98926-3917
January 25, 2009 -- 3:30 -- 4:00 PM

OUR RELATIONSHIP TO CIVIL AUTHORITIES

I. INTRODUCTION: God is the author of order, not anarchy. Paul here is not arguing for any particular order of government, but simple of government and order. Moreover he is against all lawlessness and disorder. The Apostle Peter does essentially the same. The only time we are to disobey the laws of our government is when those laws violate God's laws. In (Acts 5:29) the Apostle Peter responded to the authorities with these words: "We ought to obey God rather than men."

TEXT: "Let every soul be subject unto the higher powers. For there is no power but of God: the powers that be are ordained of God. (2) Whosoever therefore resisteth the power, resisteth the ordinance of God: and they that resist shall receive to themselves damnation. (3) For rulers are not a terror to good works, but to the evil. Wilt thou then not be afraid of the power? do that which is good, and thou shalt have praise of the same. (4) For he is the minister of God to thee for good. But if thou do that which is evil, be afraid; for he beareth not the sword in vain: for he is the minister of God, a revenger to execute wrath upon him that doeth evil. (5) Wherefore ye must needs be subject, not only for wrath, but also for conscience sake. (6) For this cause pay ye tribute also: for they are God's ministers, attending continually upon this very thing. (7) Render therefore to all their dues: tribute to whom tribute is due; custom to whom custom; fear to whom fear; honour to whom honour." (Romans 13:1-7)

(I Peter 2: 13-20) "Submit yourselves to every ordinance of man for the Lord's sake: whether it be to the king, as supreme; (14) Or unto governors, as unto them that are sent by him for the punishment of evildoers, and for the praise of them that do well. (15) For so is the will of God, that with well-doing ye may put to silence the ignorance of foolish men: (16) As free, and not using your liberty for a cloak of maliciousness, (as a cover-up for evil) but as the servants of God. (17) Honour (show proper respect to everyone) all men. Love the brotherhood. Fear God. Honour the king. (18) Servants, be subject to your masters with all fear; not only to the good and gentle, but also to the froward (those who are harsh). (19) For this is thankworthy, if a man for conscience toward God endure grief, suffering wrongfully. (20) For what glory is it, if, when ye be buffeted for your faults, ye shall take it patiently? but if, when ye do well, and suffer for it, ye take it patiently, this is acceptable with God. (21) For even hereunto were ye called: because Christ also suffered for us, leaving us an example, that ye should follow his steps: (22) Who did no sin, neither was guile found in his mouth: (23) Who, when he was reviled, reviled not again; when he suffered, he threatened not; but committed himself to him that judgeth righteously: (24) Who his own self bare our sins in his own body on the tree, that we, being dead to sins, should live unto righteousness: by whose stripes ye were healed. (25) For ye were as sheep going astray; but are now returned unto the Shepherd and Bishop of your souls."

HEARTHSTONE COTTAGE

Ellensburg, WA 98926-3917
February 22, 2009 -- 3:30 -- 4:00 PM

DAVID'S PRAYER AFTER HIS GREAT SIN

TEXT: "Create in me a clean heart, O God; and renew a right spirit within me. Cast me not away from thy presence; and take not thy holy spirit from me. Restore unto me the joy of thy salvation; and uphold me with thy free spirit." (Psalms 51:10-12)

INTRODUCTION: This Psalm is often called "THE SINNER'S GUIDE". And rightly so, as the Bible very clearly declares that ALL humanity have sinned and therefore need God's gracious cleansing and forgiveness. Moreover, it portrays or presents the right heart attitude for becoming right with God.

I. **DAVID'S PENITENCE AND PLEA FOR PARDON**: Psalm 51:1-12

   A. David's plea for mercy and pardon (vs. 1ff.)

      1. Note David offers no excuse nor self-justification.
      2. David appeals to God's love and mercy, he only admits his transgression.
      3. He admits his sin (iniquity) pleads for thorough cleansing. (vs. 3-4)

(NOTE: David confesses that his sin is first and foremost against GOD! (vs. 4)

    4. David admits the reality of human inborn sin (vs. 5), and acknowledges the virtues God desires. (vs. 6)

    5. (vs. 7-9) David continues to pray for pardon and cleansing.

       (a) "Purge" me, "wash" me - whiter than snow. (vs. 7)

       (b) He longs for joy and gladness, rather than a crushed and broken spirit. (vs. 8)

       (c) Again David pleas for God's forgiveness, "blot out all mine iniquities" (vs. 9)

B. After David's prayer for mercy, pardon, forgiveness, he longs for a new relationship with God.

    1. "Create in me a clean heart, O God; and renew a right spirit within me." (vs. 10)

    2. "Cast me not away from thy presence; and take not thy Holy Spirit from me."(11)

    3. "Restore unto me the joy of thy salvation; and uphold me with thy free spirit."

II. **THE EFFECTIVE RESULT OR FRUIT OF DIVINE FORGIVENESS**: (13-17)

A. O the joy of sins forgiven! (vs. 13-17)

    1. "Then"! David could teach others and sinners would be converted. (vs. 13)

    2. Upon deliverance from sin, David would sing of God's righteousness. (vs. 14)

    3. He pleads for God's help in order to adequately praise God. (vs. 15, 16)

    4. The sacrifices God desires:

        (a) "a broken spirit"

        (b) "a broken and a contrite spirit"

III. **CONCLUSION**: The attitude and spirit of David in this Psalm may be applied to every human being. For the Bible says, "For all have sinned, and come short of the glory of God." (Romans 3:23) And again, "As it is written, There is none righteous, no, not one." (Romans 3:10) And again, "The fool hath said in his heart, There is no God. They are corrupt, they have done abominable works, there is none that doeth good. The Lord looked down from heaven upon the children of men, to see if there were any that did understand, and seek God. They are all gone aside, they are all together become filthy; there is none that doeth good, no, not one." (Psalms 14:1-3)

HEARTHSTONE COTTAGE

Ellensburg, WA 98926
April 25, 2009 -- 3:30 -- 4:00 P.M.

GOD'S KNOWLEDGE OF ALL HUMANITY

TEXT: "O Lord, thou hast searched me, and known me. (2) Thou knowest my downsitting and mine uprising, thou understandest my thought afar off. (3) Thou compassest my path and my lying down, and art acquainted with all my ways. (4) For there is not a word in my tongue, but, lo, O Lord, thou knowest it altogether." (Psalms 139:1-4)

INTRODUCTION: The reality that the eternal living God knows everything about each and every human being is clearly declared in Holy Scripture. Nothing is hidden from His eyes. To all who do not want God to know all about them this may be distressing. But to all true children of God His perfect knowledge of them is comforting.

I. **JESUS KNEW WHAT WAS IN MAN:** "But Jesus did not commit himself unto them, because he knew all men. And needed not that any should testify of man: for he knew what was in man." (John 2:24, 25)

    A. "And Jesus knowing their thoughts said, Wherefore think ye evil in your hearts?" (Matthew 9:4)

    B. "And immediately when Jesus perceived in his spirit that they so reasoned within themselves, he said unto them, Why reason ye these things in your hearts?" (Mark 2:8)

1. Note: This was the occasion when Jesus said to the paralytic, "Son, thy sins be forgiven thee?"

C. "But there are some of you that believe not. For Jesus knew from the beginning who they were that believed not, and who should betray him." (John 6:64)

II. <u>OTHER SCRIPTURES DECLARING GOD'S KNOWLEDGE OF ALL MEN</u>:

A. From the Old Testament . . .

1. "The Lord knoweth the thoughts of man, that they are vanity." (Psalms 94:11)
2. "The thoughts of the wicked are an abomination to the Lord:" (Prov. 15:26a)
3. The prophet Isaiah declares: "For I know their works and their thoughts:" (Isaiah 66:18a)
4. Job declared: "For His eyes are upon the ways of man, and He seeth all his goings." (Job 34:21)
5. Solomon by Divine inspiration said: " For the ways of man are before the eyes of the Lord, and he pondereth (examines) all his goings." (Proverbs 5:21)
6. Again from Proverbs: "The eyes of the Lord are in every place, beholding the evil and the good." (Proverbs 15:3)
7. God speaking through the prophet Jeremiah says: "For mine eyes are upon all their ways: they are not hid from my face, neither is their iniquity hid from mine eyes." (Jeremiah 16:17)
8. Again from Jeremiah: "Ah Lord God! behold, thou hast made the heaven and the earth by thy great power and stretched out arm, and there is nothing too hard for thee: . . . Great in counsel, and mighty in work: for thine eyes are open upon all the ways of the sons

of men: to give every one according to his ways, and according to the fruit of his doings:" (Jeremiah 32:17, 19)

9. "For the eyes of the Lord run to and fro throughout the whole earth, to show himself strong in the behalf of them whose heart is perfect toward him." (2 Chronicles 16:9a)

III. <u>A PERSONAL PRAYER FOR GOD TO SEARCH MY HEART</u>:

A. "Search **me**, O God, and know **my** heart: try **me**, and know **my** thoughts: And see if there be any wicked way in **me**, and lead **me** in the way everlasting." (Psalms 139:23, 24)

IV. <u>CONCLUSION:</u> Relationship with the eternal living God is a very **personal** and **individual responsibility**. No other person can believe for us, **we** must **ourselves** believe in order to know God. It is the **"whosoever"** of the Gospel. Just as another person cannot eat food for you, just so, no one else can believe for you.

Relationship with God is a very personal privilege. Jesus said, "Come unto me . . ."

HEARTHSTONE COTTAGE

Ellensburg, WA 98926
05/24/09 - 3:30 - 4:00 PM

ARE YOU HUNGRY AND THIRSTY FOR GOD?

TEXT: "As the hart panteth after the water brooks, so panteth my soul after thee, O God. My soul thirsteth for God, for the living God: when shall I come and appear before God?" (Psalms 42:1-2)

INTRODUCTION: One of the early church fathers is reported to have said of God: "Thou hast made us for Thyself, and our hearts are restless until they find rest in Thee."

It is true! God created man, His creation, to have a personal, living relationship with Him. Jesus' prayer in the garden of Gethsemane reveals God's desire for everyone, when He prayed: "And this is life eternal, that they might know thee the only true God, and Jesus Christ, whom thou hast sent." (John 17:3)

It is God who places deep within the human heart a deep desire to know and have a relationship with God. Consider the words of our text:

I. <u>THE EXPERIENCE OF THE PSALMIST DAVID:</u>

A. (Note our text)

    1. Picture the fallow deer being chased by wild dogs. He is panting for breath, weary, fearful--but more importantly, thirsty for a cool, life-giving drink of water. This is the picture David paints of himself, but in reality, it is the picture of every human soul.

        (a.) The living eternal God made man to have fellowship, sweet communion with Him. But sin destroyed that relationship. However, God so longed for man to know Him that He sent Jesus Christ to die on a cross that WHOSOEVER would call upon Him could be restored to that intimate, personal relationship with Him.

    2. NOTE: This is not just a hunger to know ABOUT God; it is a hunger to KNOW Him! Personal knowledge, personal fellowship, personal and living relationship with the eternal God! (Emphasize again, the personal hunger and thirst for GOD Himself!)

    3. It would be well to ask ourselves the following questions:

        (a) Do I truly have a passion to KNOW God personally, intimately?

        (b) Am I willing to make the effort, take the time to KNOW God?

        (c) How important is prayer in my own life? Do I seek God daily in prayer?

        (d) Do I set aside time each day to read and meditate on God's Word?

II. CONSIDER THE WORDS OF JESUS AND THE APOSTLE PAUL"

A. "Blessed are they which do hunger and thirst after righteousness: for they shall be filled." (Matthew 5:6)

1. The Apostle Paul in his letter to the Philippian church states the passion of his life, which also should be our passion:

    (a) "But what things were gain to me, those I counted loss for Christ. Yea doubtless, and I count all things but loss for the excellency of the knowledge of Christ Jesus my Lord: for whom I have suffered the loss of all things, and do count them but dung, that I may win Christ, And be found in him, not having mine own righteousness, which is of the law, but that which is through the faith of Christ, the righteousness which is of God by Faith: **That I may know him, and the power of his resurrection, and the fellowship of his sufferings, being made conformable unto his death;** If by any means I might attain unto the resurrection of the dead." (Philippians 3:7-11)

III. **CONCLUSION**: Relationship with God is personal! Either we, personally, know God or we do not. Relationship with God is not by proxy; that is, no one else can take our place in our behalf. We, as individuals will one day stand before God and be judged on what we as one individual have done with Jesus Christ.

May we cultivate the passion that our text declares was in the heart and soul of David in the Old Testament.

"As the hart panteth after the water brooks, so panteth my soul

---

after thee, O God. My soul thirsteth for God, for the living God: when shall I come and appear before God?" (Psalms 42: 1, 2)

Be assured of this one thing: God will always satisfy the heart and soul of everyone that hungers and thirsts for Him! It is God who places the hunger and thirst deep within us and only He can satisfy our deepest need!

HEARTHSTONE COTTAGE

Ellensburg, WA 98926-3917
May 31, 2009 -- 3:30 - 4:00 PM

JESUS CHRIST -- THE GREAT "I AM"

TEXT: Various passages from John's Gospel

I. JESUS CHRIST, SENT FROM GOD:

A. "For God so loved the world, that he gave his only begotten Son, that whosoever believeth in him should not perish, but have everlasting life." (John 3:16)

1. ". . . for **I am** from him, and he hath sent me." (John 7:29b)
2. ". . . **I am** from above . . . I am not of this world." (John 8:23b)

II. "I AM THE LIGHT OF THE WORLD":

A. "**I am** the light of the world: he that followeth me shall not walk in darkness, but shall have the light of life." (John 8:12b)

1. "**I am** come a light into the world, that whosoever believeth on me should not abide in darkness." (John 12:46)

III. "I AM THE DOOR:"

A. "Then said Jesus unto them again, Verily, Verily, I say unto you, **I am** the door of the sheep. All that ever came before me are thieves and robbers: but the sheep did not hear them. **I am** the door: by me if any man enter in, he shall be saved, and shall go in and out, and find pasture. The thief cometh not, but for to steal, and to kill, and to destroy: **I am** come that they might have life, and that they might have it more abundantly." (John 10:7-10)

IV. "I AM THE GOOD SHEPHERD:"

A. "**I am** the good shepherd: the good shepherd giveth his life for the sheep." (John 10:11)

   1. "**I am** the good shepherd, and know my sheep, and am known of mine." (John 10:14)

V. "I AM THE BREAD OF LIFE:"

A. "**I am** that bread of life." (John 6:48)

   1. "**I am** the living bread which came down from heaven: if any man eat of this bread, he shall live forever: and the bread that I will give is my flesh, which I will give for the life of the world." (John 6:51)

   2. "And Jesus said unto them, **I am** the bread of life: he that cometh to me shall never hunger; and he that believeth on me shall never thirst." (John 6:35)

VI. "I AM THE WAY, THE TRUTH, AND THE LIFE:"

A. "Jesus saith unto him, **I am** the way, the truth, and the life: no man cometh unto the Father, but by me." (John 14:6)

VII. "I AM THE TRUE VINE, AND MY FATHER IS THE HUSBANDMAN."

A. "**I am** the vine, ye are the branches; he that abideth in me, and I in him, the same bringeth forth much fruit: for without me ye can do nothing." (John 15:5)

VIII. "I AM ALPHA AND OMEGA"

A. "**I am** Alpha and Omega, the beginning and the ending, saith the Lord, which is, and which was, and which is to come, the Almighty." (Revelation 1:8)

1. "**I am** Alpha and Omega, the first and the last:" (Revelation 1:11a)
2. " . . . Fear not; **I am** the first and the last:" (Revelation 1:17b)
3. "**I am** he that liveth, and was dead; and, behold, **I am** alive for evermore, Amen; and have the keys of hell and of death." (Revelation 1:18)

IX. **CONCLUSION**: From these passages of inspired Scripture God has given us the reality of who and what Jesus Christ can be to every person who will come to Him. Jesus said:

"**I am** from above"
"**I am** not of this world"
"**I am** the light of the world."
"**I am** the door."
"**I am** the good shepherd."
"**I am** the bread of life."
"**I am** the way, the truth, and the life."
"**I am** the true vine.
"**I am** Alpha and Omega, the beginning and the ending, saith the

Lord, which is, and which was, and which is to come, the Almighty." (Revelation 1:8)

"**I am** Alpha and Omega, the first and the last."

"Fear not**, I am** the first and the last."

"**I am** he that liveth, and was dead; and, behold**, I am** alive forevermore, Amen; and have the keys of hell and of death."

HEARTHSTONE COTTAGE

Ellensburg, WA 98926-3917
July 26, 2009 -- 3:30 -- 4:00 PM

GOD'S GRACIOUS INVITATION TO COME TO HIM

TEXT: "Come now, and let us reason together, saith the Lord: though your sins be as scarlet, they shall be as white as snow; though they be red like crimson, they shall be as wool." (Isaiah 1:18)

INTRODUCTION: When the Apostle Peter--a Jew--was in the house of Cornelius—a Gentile--he spoke these words: " . . . Of a truth I perceive that God is no respecter of persons." (Acts 10:34b). It is true; nationality, color of skin, language spoken, station in life, male or female, rich or poor---any, and all who will come to God may do so. The Divine invitation is open and given to "whosoever will".

The Apostle Peter also declares in his first letter (speaking of God): ". . . who without respect of persons judgeth according to every man's work, . . . " (I Peter 1:17b)

I. CONSIDER THE WORDS OF JESUS:

A. "Come unto me, all ye that labor and are heavy laden, and I will give you rest. Take my yoke upon you, and learn of me; for I am meek and lowly in heart: and ye shall find rest unto your souls. For my yoke is easy, and my burden is light." (Matthew 11:28-30)

170

1. "I am come that they might have life, and that they might have it more abundantly." (John 10:10b)

2. "For God so loved the world, that he gave his only begotten Son, that whosoever believeth in him should not perish, but have everlasting life. For God sent not His Son into the world to condemn the world; but that the world through him might be saved. He that believeth on him is not condemned: but he that believeth not is condemned already, because he hath not believed in the name of the only begotten Son of God." (John 3:16-18)

3. "But whosoever drinketh of the water that I shall give him shall never thirst; but the water that I shall give him shall be in him a well of water springing up into everlasting life." (John 4:14)

4. "I am the door: by me if any man enter in, he shall be saved, and shall go in and out, and find pasture. The thief cometh not, but for to steal, and to kill, and to destroy; I am come that they might have life, and that they might have it more abundantly." (John 10:9-10)

II. THE MINISTRY OF THE APOSTLES:

A. Peter, on the Day of Pentecost declared to all those present: "And it shall come to pass, that whosoever shall call on the name of the Lord shall be saved." (Acts 2:21)

1. Peter, at the house of Cornelius: " . . .Of a truth I perceive that God is no respecter of persons . . ." (Acts 10:34b)

B. Paul, the Apostle: "For whosoever shall call on the name of the Lord shall be saved." (Romans 10:13)

C. John, the revelator on the Isle of Patmos: "And the Spirit and the bride say, Come. And let him that heareth say, Come. And let him that is athirst come. And whosoever will, let him take the water of life freely." (Revelation 22:17)

III. <u>CONCLUSION:</u> **It is never the desire or will of God that any person not know the living God. Note, our text! Again, "whosoever" will may come!**

HEARTHSTONE COTTAGE

Ellensburg, WA 98926-3917
August 23, 2009 -- 3:30 - 4:00 PM

GOD'S DESIRE FOR EVERY LIVING PERSON

TEXT "The Lord is not slack concerning his promise, as some men count slackness; but is longsuffering to us-ward, not willing that any should perish, but that all should come to repentance." (2 Peter 3:9)

I. **INTRODUCTION**: Centuries before Jesus Christ came into this world, the Psalmist declared: "But thou, O Lord, art a God full of compassion, and gracious, longsuffering, and plenteous in mercy and truth." (Psalms 86:15)

Note the similarity between the Old and New Testaments in these passages of Scripture.

II. **THE ETERNAL CHANGELESS GOD SEEKS LOST HUMANITY**:

A. Jesus Christ came to save the lost.

1. "For the Son of man is come to seek and to save that which was lost." (Luke 19:10) Apart from God, every human being needs a Saviour!

2. God's desire has ever been to save lost humanity. Malachi, the last OLD TESTAMENT prophet declared: "For I am the Lord, I change not; . . ." (Malachi 3:6a)

   (a) The Bible declares: "God is not a man, that he should lie; neither the son of man, that he should repent: hath he said, and shall he not do it? or hath he spoken, and shall he not make it good?" (Numbers 23:19)

[1] In this regard, the NEW TESTAMENT apostle James says of God: ". . . with whom there is no variableness, neither shadow of turning." (James 1:17b) That is, like shifting shadows ever changing. God does not change---He longs for ALL to be saved.

B. The Apostle Paul in writing to Timothy declared of God: "Who will have all men to be saved, and to come unto the knowledge of the truth." (I Timothy 2:4)

   1. Consider the OLD TESTAMENT prophet, Ezekiel: "Say unto them, As I live, saith the Lord God, I have no pleasure in the death of the wicked; but that the wicked turn from his way and live: turn ye, turn ye from your evil ways; for why will ye die, O house of Israel?" (Ezekiel 33:11)

I. **CONCLUSION:** God has made marvelous and wonderful promises; but we humans have the responsibility to respond to what God has promised. Jesus Christ gave the gracious invitation: "Come unto me, all ye that labour and are heavy laden, and I will give you rest. Take my yoke upon you, and learn of me; for I am meek and lowly in heart: and ye shall find rest unto your souls. For my yoke is easy, and my burden is light." (Matthew 11:28-30)

HEARTHSTONE COTTAGE

Ellensburg, WA 98926-3917
September 26, 2009 - 3:30 - PM

THE MEASURE OF LOVE

TEXT: John 15:9-17 Note esp. vs. 12, 13, 17: "This is my commandment, That ye love one another, as I have loved you. Greater love hath no man than this, that a man lay down his life for his friends. . . These things I command you, that ye love one another." (John 15:12, 13, 17)

INTRODUCTION: On October 2, 1954, First Lieutenant James O. Conway took off from Boston Logan Airport, flying a plane carrying a load of ammunition (explosives). When his plane became airborne, he suddenly lost power. In an instant, Conway faced a brutal choice---eject from the plane and save his own life, thus allowing the plane to crash into an East Boston neighborhood, killing many people---or stay with the plane and crash it into the bay, thus giving his own life for the sake of others. His decision was to stay with the plane---thus giving his life to save others. NOTE: In simple terms, this is what Jesus Christ did for us---He gave his life that we might have eternal life!

I. <u>THE GOLDEN TEXT OF THE BIBLE</u>:

A. "For God so loved the world, that he gave his only begotten Son, that whosoever believeth in him should not perish, but have everlasting life" (John 3:16) . . .

B. That God has loved us cannot be called in question---the greater issue for us is --- what will we do in response to God's love for us?

    1. We are given the choice---reject God's love in Christ . . . or respond by

    2. surrendering our lives to Him

II. <u>THE MEASURE OF LOVE:</u>

A. Someone once said: "the measure of love is what one is willing to give up for it ".

    1. God loved us ---you---me, every human being, so much that He willingly gave up His only Son, that whosoever would receive that love might have everlasting life

    2. So the question becomes: "What am I willing to give up to follow the Lord Jesus....who gave His life for me?" Will I give up the following?:

        a. My pre-conceived ideas and beliefs . . .

        b. My sins of pride, selfishness, hatred of someone, wrong or lustful desires, love of prideful attitudes, love of "things", . . .the list goes on---in short, anything that might keep me from truly following and loving the Lord Jesus.

B. Shortly before His ascension to the Father, Jesus asked Peter three (3) times, "Peter, do you love me?"

   1. The question Jesus asked Peter might well be asked of each one of us today!

"DO YOU LOVE ME?"

III. **CONCLUSION**: Jesus said: "He that hath my commandments, and keepeth them, he it is that loveth me: and he that loveth me shall be loved of my father, and I will love him, and will manifest myself to him." (John 14:21)

QUESTION: Each one of us need to ask ourselves:
DO I LOVE THE LORD JESUS?

HEARTHSTONE COTTAGE,

Ellensburg, WA - 98926-3917
October 25, 2009 -- 3:30 - 4:00 PM

JESUS SAID, "I AM THE DOOR"

TEXT: ". . . Verily, verily, I say unto you, I am the door of the sheep. I am the door: by me if any man enter in, he shall be saved, and shall go in and out, and find pasture." (John 10:7b, 9) See -- context: (John 10:1-11)

INTRODUCTION: Jesus often used very simple, very common words to present the truth. What could be more easily understood than to use the word "door"? A door gives us entrance to a house, a building, a room, etc. We even use this very common word in other ways: Luke, the writer of the book of Acts and traveling companion of the Apostle Paul, says in Acts 14:27; "And when they were come, and had gathered the church together, they rehearsed all that God had done with them, and how he had opened the door of faith to the Gentiles." In the text before us, Jesus uses the word "door" to declare that HE is the "entrance" or "door"; to a vital and living relationship with God. Note again the words of our text: (John 10:7b, 9).

I. "I AM THE DOOR OF THE SHEEP:

A. One "way" to God! And Jesus Christ is that way.

1. "Neither is there salvation in any other: for there is none other name under heaven given among men, whereby we must be saved." (Acts 4:12)

2. "Jesus saith unto him, I am the way, the truth, and the life: no man cometh unto the Father, but by me." (John 14:6) Jesus was responding to Thomas who had said, "Lord, we know not whither thou goest; and how can we know the way?" (John 14:5)]

3. Even before Jesus Christ came into our world this message was the same. The Angel of the Lord came to Joseph, the husband of Mary, to reassure him that it was right for him to take Mary as his wife (even though she was expecting a child before their marriage). The angel said, "And she shall bring forth a son, and thou shalt call his name JESUS: for he shall save his people from their sins." (Matthew 1:21)

   (a) God's Word further explains: "Now all this was done, that it might be fulfilled which was spoken of the Lord by the prophet saying, Behold, a virgin shall be with child, and shall bring forth a son, and they shall call his name Emmanuel, which being interpreted is, God with us." (Matthew 1:22-23)

B. When Peter was preaching to Cornelius, the Roman official, he declared, "To him give all the prophets witness, that through his name whosoever believeth in him shall receive remission of sins." (Acts 10:43)

II. JESUS CHRIST, THE DOOR, GIVES ABUNDANT LIFE TO THOSE WHO RECEIVE HIM:

A. Note the words of Jesus in our text: "The thief cometh not, for to steal, and to kill, and to destroy: I am come that they might have life, and that they might have it more abundantly." (John 10:10)

1. Jesus Christ invites all to come to Him. "Come unto me, all ye that labour and are heavy laden, and I will give you rest. Take my yoke upon you, and learn of me; for I am meek and lowly in heart: and ye shall find rest unto your souls. For my yoke is easy, and my burden is light." (Matthew 11:28-30)

B. The message of John the Baptist: "The next day John seeth Jesus coming unto him, and saith, Behold the Lamb of God, which taketh away the sin of the world." (John 1:29)

III. **CONCLUSION**: The message of the Gospel of Jesus Christ is very simple. Too often people confuse it by injecting human logic and reasoning. Again, it was Jesus who said, "Verily I say unto you, Except ye be converted, and become as little children, ye shall not enter into the kingdom of heaven," (Mathew 18:3)

As noted earlier in this message, we must "learn" of Him. He is the Lord, our creator, the "one" and "only" saviour, the eternal living God.

Again, the words of the Apostle Peter before the Jewish council: "Neither is there salvation in any other: for there is none other name under heaven given among men, whereby we must be saved." (Acts 4:12)

HEARTHSTONE COTTAGE

Ellensburg, WA 98926-3917
November 22, 2009 - 3:30 - 4:00 PM

BE THANKFUL UNTO HIM

TEXT: Psalm 100: esp. verse 4: **"Enter into his gates with thanksgiving, and into his courts with praise: be thankful unto him, and bless his name."**

INTRODUCTION: Manifesting or demonstrating a "thankful" heart and life is simply living in obedience to God. The old song, "Count Your Blessings", is not only good to sing--it also is good advice for happy victorious living--as well as pleasing God.

I. CONSIDER THE OLD TESTAMENT SCRIPTURAL ADMONITION TO BE THANKFUL:

A. Besides Psalms **100, consider the following Scriptural commands and promises:**

   1. "Praise ye the Lord. O give **thanks** unto the Lord; for he is good: for his mercy endureth for ever." (Psalms 106:1)

   2. "O come, let us sing unto the Lord: let us make a joyful noise to the Rock of our salvation. Let us come before his presence with **thanksgiving,** and make a joyful noise unto him with psalms." (Psalms 95:1, 2)

---

3. "Sing unto the Lord with **thanksgiving**; sing praise upon the harp unto our God." **(Psalms 147:7)**
4. "I will praise the name of God with a song, and will magnify him with **thanksgiving**." (Psalms 69:30)
5. "Offer unto God **thanksgiving**; and pay thy vows unto the most High:" (Psalms 50:14)
6. "I will offer to thee the sacrifice of **thanksgiving**, and will call upon the name of the Lord." (Psalms 116:17)
7. "O give **thanks** unto the Lord; for he is good: for his mercy endureth forever. O give **thanks** unto the God of gods: for his mercy endureth forever. O give **thanks** to the Lord of lords: for his mercy endureth forever." (Psalms 136:1-3)
8. "Give **thanks** unto the Lord, call upon his name, make known his deeds among the people." (I Chronicles 16:8)

II. ALSO THE NEW TESTAMENT COMMANDS FOR THANKFULNESS:

A. From the Pauline Epistles:

1. "In everything give **thanks**: for this is the will of God in Christ Jesus concerning you." (I Thessalonians 5:18)
2. "Continue in prayer, and watch in the same with **thanksgiving**;" (Colossians 4:2)
3. "Giving **thanks** always for all things unto God and the Father, in the name of our Lord Jesus Christ;" (Ephesians 5:20)
4. "Be careful (anxious) for nothing; but in everything by prayer and supplication with **thanksgiving** let your requests be made know unto God." (Philippians 4:6)
5. "As ye have therefore received Christ Jesus the Lord, so walk ye in him: Rooted and built up in him, and stablished in the faith, as ye have been taught,

abounding therein with **thanksgiving**." (Colossians 2:6, 7)

6. "And let the peace of God rule in your hearts, to the which also ye are called in one body; and be ye **thankful**." (Colossians 3:15)

7. "**Thanks** be unto God for his unspeakable (indescribable) gift." (2 Corinthians 9:15)

HEARTHSTONE COTTAGE

Ellensburg, WA 98926-3917
January 24, 2010 - 3:30 - 4:00 PM

GOD IS WORTHY OF OUR PRAISE

TEXT: Psalms 147:1ff.

INTRODUCTION: Significantly, Psalms 146 - 150, begin and end with the words, "Praise ye the Lord." Or it can be translated, Hallelujah! If we would but realize that every good thing we have comes from God, we would praise Him more! It was the Apostle James who declared: "Every good gift and every perfect gift is from above, and cometh down from the Father of lights, with whom there is no variableness, neither shadow of turning." (James 1:17)

I. **GOD IS WORTHY OF OUR PRAISE AND THANKFULNESS**

A. PAY Him we cannot, but Praise Him we can!

1. Note that it is good because it is right, good because it is acceptable with God and also beneficial to ourselves.
2. Again, the Psalmist declared, Psalms 107:8, 15, 21, 31, these words: "Oh that men would praise the Lord for his goodness, and for his wonderful works to the children of men."

B. Consider some reasons for giving heartfelt praise to God: (Psalms 147:3) "He healeth the broken in heart, and bindeth up their wounds."

    1. Followed by this the Psalmist declares in vs. 4: "He telleth the number of the stars; He calleth them all by their names."

    2. Vs. 5 further exalts the power and wisdom of our God: "Great is our Lord, and of great power: His understanding is infinite."

II. **MORE REASONS TO GIVE THANKS AND PRAISE TO GOD:** (vs. 7-9, 11)

A. (vs. 7) Consider the Psalmist's words in Psalms 104:33,34.

"I will sing unto the Lord as long as I live: I will sing praise to my God while I have my being. My meditation of him shall be sweet: I will be glad in the Lord."

B. Note the care and concern God gives regarding His creation and the creatures upon it: (vs. 8, 9) "Who covereth the heaven with clouds, who prepareth rain for the earth, who maketh grass to grow upon the mountain. He giveth to the beast his food, and to the young ravens which cry."

III. **CONCLUSION**: When God's Word declares His concern for the earth and the creatures upon it; do you not think that God thinks and cares about you? Jesus said,

"Wherefore, if God so clothe the grass of the field, which today is, and tomorrow is cast into the oven, shall He not much more clothe you, O ye of little faith?" (Matthew 6:30)

HEARTHSTONE COTTAGE

Ellensburg, WA 98926
MARCH 28, 2010 -- 3:30 - 4:00 PM

THE PRAYER EVERYONE SHOULD PRAY

TEXT: Search me, O God, and know my heart: try me, and know my thoughts. And see if there be any wicked way in me, and lead me in the way everlasting." (Psalms 139:23, 24)

I. **INTRODUCTION:** It is right and proper for Christians to pray for fellow believers and for people who do not know the Lord that they might come to know the Saviour, Jesus Christ. In fact, it is our Christian and spiritual duty. But we should also remember that it is also right to pray for OURSELVES! Notice the prayer of the Psalmist in the text before us

II. **"SEARCH ME, O GOD, AND KNOW MY HEART**. . ." (vs. 23a)

    A. Why should we ask God to do what he already knows about us?

        1. The beginning verses of this chapter make clear that God already knew the heart of the Psalmist. (See, vs. 1ff)

        2. Therefore our asking God to search our hearts, demonstrates a seeking, humble and obedient

heart attitude. It also indicates an heart desiring to please God.

III. 'TRY ME, AND KNOW MY THOUGHTS. . ." (VS. 23b)

A. Note again the words of the Psalmist in vs. 2: "Thou knowest my downsitting and mine uprising, thou understandest my thought afar off."

    1. Words come from thoughts; therefore, we need to keep our thoughts clean and right in His sight.

    2. Again, our willingness to have God KNOW us and TRY us indicates desire on our part to do what is right in God's sight. Remember, God already knows all about us, including our thoughts and desires. But our asking Him to do this, that is, search us and try us, places us in the position to change and become right in His sight.

IV. "AND SEE IF THERE BE ANY WICKED WAY IN ME. . ." (vs. 24a.)

A. The prayer of the Psalmist is a prayer that all of us can and should pray. For someday we ALL shall stand before God in judgment.

    1. "For we must all appear before the judgment seat of Christ; that every one may receive the things done in his body, according to that he hath done, whether it be good or bad." (2 Corinthians 5:10)

B. Openness of heart and life before God is absolutely essential for a close walk with God. Known sin, allowed to remain in our lives always separates us from a close walk with God. That is why the Bible declares: "If we confess our sins, he is faithful and just to forgive us our sins, and to cleanse us from all unrighteousness." (I John 1:9)

V. "**AND LEAD ME IN THE WAY EVERLASTING**. . ." (vs. 24b).

    A. Note again, the prayer for "me"; for we will not be of any real help to others unless we are in right relationship with God ourselves.

        1. The Good Shepherd longs to give everyone life now and eternal life with Him forever. Jesus said in John 10:11, 14, "I am the good shepherd: the good shepherd giveth his life for the sheep. . . I am the good shepherd, and know my sheep, and am known of mine."

CONCLUSION: Jesus said, "Come unto me," and "I am the door." COME TODAY!"

HEARTHSTONE COTTAGE

Ellensburg, WA 98926-3917
April 25, 2010 - 3:30 - 4:00 PM

THE DIVINE INVITATION
TO ALL MANKIND

TEXT: "Come unto me, all ye that labour and are heavy laden, and I will give you rest." also . . . "Come now, and let us reason together, saith the Lord: though your sins be as scarlet, they shall be as white as snow; though they be red like crimson, they shall be as wool." (Matthew 11:28; Isaiah 1:18)

I. INTRODUCTION: Throughout the Bible, it is God who comes seeking man. It was so in the Garden of Eden after Adam and Eve had sinned. In the cool of the day, God called to Adam, "And they heard the voice of the Lord God walking in the garden in the cool of the day: and Adam and his wife hid themselves from the presence of the Lord God amongst the trees of the garden. And the Lord God called unto Adam, and said unto him, Where art thou?" (Genesis 3:8, 9) Though humans, (people) have sinned against God, it still is God who comes seeking man.

II. "COME UNTO ME"

A. Human nature still responds in the same way. (Illus. of our children when they had not done right, had disobeyed.)

1. We are the ones who have failed; yet it is God who comes seeking to restore the broken relationship. The One sinned against, seeks out the sinner.
2. Adam and Eve hid themselves. But this is impossible, for God will always find us. Far better that we come to Him, confess our sins, our wrongdoing and ask for His forgiveness. God longs to restore a broken relationship!
3. Running from God will never give us peace or make us happy. Far better, when we have failed God---that we run TO Him. (Note our text) "Come unto me . . .
4. Running into the arms of God will always bring untold blessings.

    (a) "If ye be willing and obedient, ye shall eat the good of the land." (Isaiah 1:19)

(Note: Blessings depend upon our being willing to come to our God).

    (b) "The Lord is not slack concerning his promise, as some men count slackness; but is longsuffering to usward, not willing that any should perish, but that all should come to repentance." (II Peter 3:9)

III. BLESSING OF COMING TO GOD:

A. The burden of sin can be taken away.

1. A living relationship with the living God can be ours, every day, every hour, every moment of the day. This is what God longs to give; but we MUST come,
2. Our load, the burden of sin can be gone in a moment.
3. We sing the song, "What can wash away my sin, nothing but the blood of Jesus."
4. A living relationship with God can be ours! He longs to be our Heavenly Father in a very personal way.

IV. **<u>CONCLUSION</u>:** Have you come to Him? Has He saved you from your sins? He longs to forgive and restore a living relationship with "whosoever will". God has no special pets or favorites. He is no respecter of persons. If you do not know Him as your own personal Saviour, then ask Him NOW to come into your heart. He longs to save "whosoever will" call upon His name. For His promise is, "whosoever shall call upon the name of the Lord shall be saved." (Acts 2:21b)

HEARTHSTONE COTTAGE

Ellensburg, WA 98926-3917
May 23, 2010 -- 3:30 - 4:00 PM

THE POWER AND IMPORTANCE
OF GOD'S WORD

TEXT: "Sanctify them through thy truth: thy word is truth."
(John 17:17)

I. INTRODUCTION: The importance and POWER of the
Word of God cannot be over-emphasized! When Moses was
speaking to the Israelites in the wilderness before they had
even seen the promised land, Moses said these words: "And he
humbled thee, and suffered thee to hunger, and fed thee with
manna, which thou knewest not, neither did thy fathers know;
that he might make thee know that man doth not live by bread
only, but by every word that proceedeth out of the mouth of
the Lord doth man live."

('Deuteronomy 8:3) I want to give you a number of passages from
God's Word today which emphasize the power and importance of
God's written Word.

II. <u>DO NOT TAMPER OR CHANGE GOD'S WORD:</u>

A. "Now therefore hearken, O Israel, unto the statutes and unto the judgments, which I teach you, for to do them, that ye may live, and go in and possess the land which the Lord God of your fathers giveth you. Ye shall not add unto the word which I command you, neither shall ye diminish ought from it, that ye may keep the commandments of the Lord your God which I command you." (Deuteronomy 4:1-2)

1. Jesus Christ set the example for us during His temptation by Satan in the wilderness. "And when he had fasted forty days and forty nights, he was afterward an hungered. And when the tempter came to him, he said, If thou be the Son of God, command that these stones be made bread. But he (Jesus) answered and said, It is written, Man shall not live by bread alone, but by every word that proceedeth out of the mouth of God." (Matthew 4:2-4)

2. "As for God, his way is perfect; the word of the Lord is tried: he is a buckler to all them that trust in him." (2 Samuel 22:31)

III. <u>NEW TESTAMENT EMPHASIS OT GOD'S WORD:</u>

A. "As newborn babes, desire the sincere milk of the word, that ye may grow thereby: If so be ye have tasted that the Lord is gracious." (I Peter 2:2-3)

1. "Seeing ye have purified your souls in obeying the truth through the Spirit unto unfeigned love of the brethren, see that ye love one another with a pure heart fervently: Being born again, not of corruptible seed, but of incorruptible, by the word of God, which

liveth and abideth for ever. For all flesh is as grass, and all the glory of man as the flower of grass. The grass withereth, and the flower thereof falleth away: But the word of the Lord endureth forever. And this is the word which by the gospel is preached unto you." (I Peter 1:22-25)

2. "We have also a more sure word of prophecy; whereunto ye do well that ye take heed, as unto a light that shineth in a dark place, until the day dawn, and the day star arise in our hearts: Knowing this first, that no prophecy of the scripture is of any private interpretation. For the prophecy came not in old time by the will of man: but holy men of God spake as they were moved by the Holy Ghost." (2 Peter 1:19-21)

IV. <u>OLD TESTAMENT EMPHASIS OF GOD'S WORD:</u>

A. "The law of the Lord is perfect, converting the soul: the testimony of the Lord is sure, making wise the simple. The statutes of the Lord are right, rejoicing the heart: the commandment of the Lord is pure, enlightening the eyes. The fear of the Lord is clean, enduring for cver: the judgments of the Lord are true and righteous altogether." (Psalms 19:7-9)

B. "For the Lord is good; his mercy is everlasting; and his truth endureth to all generations." (Psalms 100:5)

C. "For his merciful kindness is great toward us: and the truth of the Lord endureth for ever. Praise ye the Lord." (Psalms 117:2)

D. "Forever, O Lord, thy word is settled in heaven." (Psalms 119:89)

E. "Thy word is a lamp unto my feet, and a light unto my path." (Psalms 119:105)

F. "The entrance of thy words giveth light; it giveth understanding unto the simple." (Psalms 119:130)

G. "Thy word is true from the beginning: and every one of thy righteous judgments endueth forever." (Psalms 119:160)

V. **CONCLUSION:** The importance of the Word of God cannot be over-emphasized. Let it be bread to your soul and water to your spirit. Let it direct your steps in order to please God! THY WORD IS TRUE!

HEARTHSTONE COTTAGE

Ellensburg, WA 98926-3917
June 27, 2010 - 3:30 - 4:00 PM

THE ETERNAL, LIVING
GOD UNDERSTANDS

TEXT: "In all their affliction he was afflicted, and the angel of his presence saved them: in his love and in his pity he redeemed them; and he bare them, and carried them all the days of old." (Isaiah 63:9)

I. INTRODUCTION: God understands your sorrow! . . .

II. THE SORROW OF OUR LORD AND SAVIOUR:

    A. The second Gospel, Mark, tells us about the grief Jesus had because of hardened hearts; those who rejected Him, sought occasion to condemn Him. Mark tells us, He was "grieved for the hardness of their hearts," (Mark 3:5)

        1. "Jesus wept." (John 11:35)

        2. "And when he was come near, he beheld the city, and wept over it, (42) Saying, If thou hadst known, even thou, at least in this thy day, the things which belong unto thy peace! but now they are hid from thine eyes. (43) For the days shall come upon thee, that thine enemies shall cast a trench about thee, and compass

thee round, and keep thee in on every side, (44) And shall lay thee even with the ground, and thy children within thee; and they shall not leave in thee one stone upon another; because thou knewest not the time of thy visitation." (Luke 19:41-44)

III. THE PAIN OF GOD, THE FATHER:

A. During the period of the Judges, when other nations were invading Israel -- because Israel had sinned against God, the Bible declares:

1. ". . . and his soul was grieved for the misery of Israel." (Judges 10:16b)
2. "How oft did they provoke him in the wilderness, and grieve him in the desert!" (Psalms 78:40)
   (a) "grieved"; that is, "be hurt or vexed"
3. The prophet Ezekiel tells how God was hurt, "broken" because of the misery His people were in (even though it was because of their sin).

   (a) "And they that escape of you shall remember me among the nations whither they shall be carried captives, because I am broken with their whorish heart, which hath departed from me, and with their eyes, which go a-whoring after their idols:" (Ezekiel 6:9b) (1) The word "broken" means to "break down, break off in pieces." Also trans. "crush". "destroy", "hurt".

B. Paul, the Apostle, declares and commands in (Ephesians 4:30) "And grieve not the holy Spirit of God, whereby ye are sealed unto the day of redemption."

IV. **CONCLUSION**: Note the words of the Psalmist: "Like as a father pitieth his children, so the Lord pitieth them that fear him." (Psalms 103:13)

Again, God's Word declares: "For we have not an high priest which cannot be touched with the feeling of our infirmities; but was in all points tempted like as we are, yet without sin." (Hebrews 4:15)

"For we do not have a high priest who is unable to sympathize with our weaknesses, but we have one who has been tempted in every way, just as we are--yet was without sin."

No wonder then that Jesus said, "Come unto me. . ."

HEARTHSTONE COTTAGE

Ellensburg, WA 98926-3917
July 25, 2010 - 3:30 - 4:00 PM

SALVATION FROM SIN FOUND IN JESUS CHRIST

TEXT: "Neither is there salvation in any other: for there is none other name under heaven given among men, whereby we must be saved." (Acts 4:12)

I. **INTRODUCTION**: The book of Acts or (Acts of the Apostles) is the history book of the New Testament. It records the beginning of what we commonly refer to as "the Church." In the Gospel of Matthew 16:18, Jesus said, "I will build my church." Later in the NEW TESTAMENT the "church" is referred to as "the body of Christ." This church is composed of "believers"; that is, those who have experienced "salvation" as found in our text.

II. **THE MEANING OF SALVATION AS USED IN THE NEW TESTAMENT**:

   A. The word "salvation" as used in the NEW TESTAMENT simply means "deliverance", or "preservation".

1. Therefore it speaks "**of the spiritual and eternal deliverance granted immediately by God to those who accept His conditions of repentance and faith in the Lord Jesus, in whom alone it is to be obtained.**" (See our text above)

B. The human need for salvation, or why do we humans need a Saviour?

　　1. "For all have sinned, and come short of the glory of God;" (Romans 3:23)
　　2. "As it is written, There is none righteous, no, not one." (Romans 3:10)

　　　　(a) Paul was declaring what the Psalmist said in (Psalms 14:1-3): "The fool hath said in his heart, There is no God. They are corrupt, they have done abominable works, there is none that doeth good. (2) The Lord looked down from heaven upon the children of men, to see if there were any that did understand, and seek God. (3) They are all gone aside, they are all together become filthy: there is none that doeth good, no, not one."

　　3. "And she shall bring forth a son, and thou shalt call his name JESUS: for he shall save his people from their sins." (Matthew 1:21)
　　4. "For there is one God, and one mediator between God and men, the man Christ Jesus; Who gave himself a ransom for all. . ." (I Timothy 2:5-6a)
　　5. John 3:16, often referred to as "the Golden text" of the Bible: "For God so loved the world, that he gave his only begotten Son, that whosoever believeth in him should not perish, but have everlasting life. For God sent not his Son into the world to condemn the world;

but that the world through him might be saved. He that believeth on him is not condemned: but he that believeth not is condemned already, because he hath not believed in the name of the only begotten Son of God." (John 3:16-18)

6. Thomas, one of Jesus' disciples asked the question-- ". . . how can we know the way?" "Jesus saith unto him, I am the way, the truth, and the life; no man cometh unto the Father, but by me." (John 14:5b-6)

7. To Martha, Lazarus' sister, "Jesus said unto her, 'I am the resurrection, and the life: he that believeth in me, though he were dead, yet shall he live: And whosoever liveth and believeth in me shall never die. Believest thou this?" (John 11:25-26)

III. <u>THE RESULT OR EFFECT OF SALVATION:</u>

A. "Therefore if any man be in Christ, he is a new creature: old things are passed away; behold, all things are become new." (2 Corinthians 5:17)

1. "But God, who is rich in mercy, for his great love wherewith he loved us, (5) Even when we were dead in sins, hath quickened us together with Christ, (by grace ye are saved;) (6) And hath raised us up together, and made us sit together in heavenly places in Christ Jesus: (7) That in the ages to come he might shew the exceeding riches of his grace in his kindness toward us through Christ Jesus. (8) For by grace are ye saved through faith; and that not of yourselves: it is the gift of God: (9) Not of works, lest any man should boast." (Ephesians 2:4-9)

(a) The Apostle Paul writing to Timothy declares of God: "Who hath saved us, and called us with an holy calling, not according to our works, but according to his own purpose and grace, which was given us in Christ Jesus before the world began." (2 Timothy 1:9)

IV. **CONCLUSION**: "Behold, I stand at the door, and knock; If any man hear my voice, and open the door, I will come in to him, and will sup with him, and he with me." (Revelation 3:20)

Again, the words of Jesus to Martha at the death of her brother Lazarus: "Jesus said unto her, I am the resurrection, and the life: he that believeth in me, though he were dead, yet shall he live; And whosoever liveth and believeth in me shall never die. Believest thou this?" (John 11:25-26)

And, the words of the Apostle Paul to Titus: "But after that the kindness and love of God our Saviour toward man appeared, Not by works of righteousness which we have done, but according to his mercy he saved us, by the washing of regeneration, and renewing of the Holy Ghost;" (Titus 3:4-5)

KITTITAS COMMUNITY CHURCH

Kittitas, WA 98934
August 08, 2010 - 11:00 AM

WORDS OF ENCOURAGEMENT TO A TROUBLED CHURCH

TEXT: "**I am the good shepherd: the good shepherd giveth his life for the sheep.** But he that is an hireling (the hired hand) and not the shepherd, whose own the sheep are not, seeth the wolf coming, and leaveth the sheep, and fleeth: and the wolf catcheth them, and scattereth the sheep. The hireling fleeth, because he is an hireling, and careth not for the sheep. **I am the good shepherd, and know my sheep, and am known of mine.**" (John 10:11-14)

I. **INTRODUCTION**: The eternal living God has compassion for every person here this morning. God has an investment in every one here this day. The cost to God was the giving of His own Son, who was sent from the glories of heaven into a world lost in sin. (John 3:16) The purpose? "For God sent not his Son into the world to condemn the world; but that the world through him might be saved." (John 3:17) Jesus said in John 10:10b, "I am come that they might have life, and that they might have it more abundantly."

II. <u>JESUS' COMMAND TO THE APOSTLE PETER</u>:

A. "Feed the flock of God which is among you, taking the oversight thereof, not by constraint, but willingly; not for filthy lucre, but of a ready mind; Neither as being lords over God's heritage, but being examples to the flock. And when the chief Shepherd shall appear, ye shall receive a crown of glory that fadeth not away." (I Peter 5:2-4)

   1. After Jesus' resurrection, He questioned Peter with these words:

      (a) "So when they had dined, Jesus saith to Simon Peter, **Simon, son of Jonas, lovest thou me more than these?** He saith unto him, Yea, Lord; thou knowest that I love thee. He saith unto him, **Feed my lambs**. He saith to him again the second time, **Simon, son of Jonas, lovest thou me?** He saith unto him, Yea, Lord; thou knowest that I love thee. He saith unto him, **Feed my sheep**. He saith unto him the third time, **Simon, son of Jonas, lovest thou me?** Peter was grieved because he said unto him the third time, **Lovest thou me?** And he said unto him, Lord, thou knowest all things; thou knowest that I love thee. Jesus saith unto him, **Feed my sheep.**" (John 21:15-17)

III. <u>PAUL'S COMMAND TO THE EPHESIAN ELDERS</u>:

A. "Take heed therefore unto yourselves, and to all the flock, over the which the Holy Ghost hath made you overseers, to feed the church of God, which he hath purchased with his own blood." (Acts 20:28)

1. God's command to the Apostle Paul to feed the church of God--applies to every minister/pastor of the Gospel today!
   (a) Paul's exhortation to the Ephesian elders: (Acts 20:17-35)

IV. **CONCLUSION:** The eternal living God has ordained the relationship between those called of God to preach/teach His Word, and the people to whom they minister. Great responsibility rests upon the minister of the Gospel to preach God's Word and guard the flock. But also, great responsibility rests upon the flock to hear and heed God's Word. God's Word is very clear: "So then every one of us shall give account of himself to God." (Romans 14:12)

Again, God's Word, the Bible, declares, "As for God, his way is perfect; the word of the Lord is tried: he is a buckler to all them that trust in him." (2 Samuel 22:31) cf. (Psalms 18:30)

Again, the Scripture declares: "He is the Rock, his work is perfect: for all his ways are judgment: a God of truth and without iniquity, just and right is he." (Deuteronomy 32:4)

HEARTHSTONE COTTAGE

Ellensburg, WA 98926-3917
August 22, 2010 -- 3:30 - 4:00

A NEW CREATURE

TEXT: "Therefore if any man be in Christ, he is a new creature: old things are passed away; behold, all things are become new." (2 Corinthians 5:17)

INTRODUCTION: GOD is the only one who can give us eternal life, for John said, "He that hath the Son hath life, and he that hath not the Son of God hath not life." (I John 5:12)

I. HOW TO BECOME -- "IN CHRIST":

    a. Acts 16:31 (Believe, faith in Christ)

    b. "For by grace are ye saved through faith; and that not of yourselves: it is the gift of God; Not of works, lest any man should boast." (Ephesians 2:8-9)

    c. "Repent" -- Luke (13:3,5) "Except ye repent, ye shall all likewise perish."

    d. "Confess sin" -- I John 1:9

        (1) Romans 3:23 - "All have sinned."

        (2) Romans 3:10 - "None righteous, no, not one."

        (3) Romans 10:9-10 - "That if thou shalt confess with thy mouth the Lord Jesus, and shalt believe

in thine heart that God has raised him from the dead, thou shalt be saved." -- "For with the heart man believeth unto righteousness; and with the mouth confession is made unto salvation." (Romans 10:9-10)

e. "Call upon the Lord" -- "For whosoever shall call upon the name of the Lord shall be saved." (Romans 10:13)

HEARTHSTONE COTTAGE

Ellensburg, WA 98926-3917
September 26, 2010 -- 3:30 -- 4:00 PM

THE PAIN OF GOD BECAUSE OF HUMAN SIN

TEXT: "How oft did they provoke him in the wilderness, and grieve him in the desert!" (Psalms 78:40) "And grieve not the Holy Spirit of God, whereby ye are sealed unto the day of redemption." (Ephesians 4:30) ("grieve" - to bring distress, to be sad, be in heaviness of heart or spirit)

INTRODUCTION: We seldom think of God experiencing "pain". Yet the Word of God declares that human sin brings pain to the heart of God. He cares about every person and He knows when we fail. Not only will we suffer if we sin, but at the same time we bring pain to the heart of God.

I. OLD TESTAMENT SCRIPTURES DECLARING GOD'S PAIN AT HUMAN SIN:

A. "How oft did they provoke him in the wilderness, and grieve him in the desert!" (Psalms 78:40)

1. "And God saw that the wickedness of man was great in the earth, and that every imagination of the thoughts of his heart was only evil continually. And it repented the

Lord that he had made man on the earth, and it grieved him at his heart." (Genesis 6:5-6)

2. " . . . and his soul was grieved for the misery of Israel." (Judges 10:16b).

3. "In all their affliction he was afflicted, and the angel of his presence saved them: in his love and in his pity he redeemed them; and he bare them, and carried them all the days of old." (Isaiah 63:9)

   (a) "But they rebelled, and vexed his Holy Spirit: therefore he was turned to be their enemy, and he fought against them." (Isaiah 63:10)

4. (The prediction of evil to come on Israel because of their sin of departing from God.) "And they that escape of you shall remember me among the nations whither they shall be carried captives, because I am broken (grieved) with their whorish heart, which hath departed from me, and with their eyes, which go a-whoring after their idols: and they shall loathe themselves for the evils which they have committed in all their abominations." (Ezekiel 6:9)

II. <u>NEW TESTAMENT SCRIPTURES DECLARING THE PAIN OF GOD:</u>

A. (Jesus weeping over Jerusalem)

1. "And when he was come near, he beheld the city, and wept over it, Saying, If thou hadst known, even thou, at least in this thy day, the things which belong unto thy peace! but now they are hid from thine eyes. For the days shall come upon thee, that thine enemies shall cast a trench about thee, and compass thee round, and keep thee in on every side, And shall lay thee even

with the ground, and thy children within thee; and they shall not leave in thee one stone upon another; because thou knewest not the time of thy visitation." (Luke 19:41-44)

I. **CONCLUSION**: "Like as a father pitieth his children, so the Lord pitieth them that fear him." (Psalms 103:13) Far better to have God's loving care for us than to experience His just judgment because of our rebellion against Him!

HEARTHSTONE COTTAGE

Ellensburg, WA 98926-3917
October 24, 2010 - 3:30 - 4:00 PM

WHAT MUST I DO TO BE SAVED?

TEXT: "... Sirs, what must I do to be saved? And they said, Believe on the Lord Jesus Christ, and thou shalt be saved, and thy house." (Acts 16:30b-31)

I. **INTRODUCTION**: The question this Philippian jailer asked Paul and Silas was/is the most important question he could ever ask, and it is also the most important question that any one of us can ask. Eternal destiny hangs on our answer to this question.

Thank God, the Bible is very clear in giving us an answer to this most important question.

II. **CONSIDER THE ANSWER OF PAUL AND SILAS:**

A. "Believe on the Lord Jesus Christ, and thou shalt be saved."

1. "believe": What a simple statement--yet so many people stumble over the simplest instructions.

(a) But people say, "I want to see something, hear something." "You know, seeing is believing."

1. The farmer sows seeds--believing they will grow.
2. You put seed in your garden, believing, expecting them to grow.
3. We expect and believe so many things in the natural realm---why not in the spiritual?

(b) Consider Paul and Silas in prison; in spite of their circumstances, they prayed and believed (trusted) God.

III. <u>GOD IS FAITHFUL</u>:

A. Paul and Silas were praising and worshipping God, possibly not even expecting the miracle that happened.

1. When we have difficulties, we often become so wrapped up in the problem that we forget God, leaving His help totally out of the picture. (Brother Ridout's advice to us)
2. **"Can't you** trust **Him?"**
3. "There hath no temptation (test) taken you but such as is common to men: but, God is faithful, who will not suffer you to be tempted (tested) above that ye are able; but will with the temptation (test) also make a way to escape, that ye may be able to bear it." (I Corinthians 10:13)

(a) Tests and trials--if we accept and endure them-- will only make us stronger.

1. **Everyone** has difficulties and heartaches. Tragically, many have no faith and trust in God! To the **believer**, God's Word declares, "And we know that all things

work together for good to them that love God, to them who are the called according to his purpose." (Romans 8:28)

2. **BUT MOST IMPORTANT OF ALL:** Do you know Jesus Christ as your personal Saviour? The Bible declares that ALL have sinned and therefore need a Saviour.

    (a) God has done His part--He sent His only Son to die that we might be saved.

3. God's Word is very clear and very simple:

"Believe on the Lord Jesus Christ;" NOT on . . . . .
. . . . .How many good deeds I must do . . .
. . . . . How much money I must pay . . .
. . . . . What church I must belong to . . .
Perhaps the list could go on and on, but the Bible is very simple: **"Believe on the Lord Jesus Christ."** In other words come to Him in simple trust and faith that He will do for you all He said He would do.

IV. **CONCLUSION:** The thief on the cross when Jesus was crucified called upon the Lord saying, "Lord, remember me. . ."

"And Jesus said unto him, "Verily I say unto thee, Today, shalt thou be with me in paradise." (Luke 23:42,43)

HEARTHSTONE COTTAGE

Ellensburg, WA 98926-3917
August 28, 2011 - 3:30 - 4:00PM
(Albert preached this sermon, one year, five months, and
fifteen days before God called him to his Heavenly Home.)

THY WORD IS TRUTH

TEXT: "Sanctify them through thy truth: thy word is truth."
(John 17:17)

"Thy word is true from the beginning: and every one of thy
righteous judgments endureth forever." (Psalms 119:160)

"Sanctify them through thy truth: thy word is truth." (John.17:17-
(*"Set apart for sacred use or make holy" (cf. vs. 19 -- Jesus'
example).*

"Thy word is true from the beginning: and every one of thy
righteous judgments endureth forever." (Psalms119:160)

I. **INTRODUCTION**: We live in a fallen world where oftentimes
    it is difficult to determine that which is true and that which is
    false. But, one thing we know, God's Word is true, and we can
    depend upon it. Perhaps the greatest problem is that we do not
    know God's Word, which is true.

II. **THE TRUTH AND POWER OF GOD'S WORD**:

    A. "Thy word have I hid in mine heart, that I might not sin
       against thee." (Psalms 119:11)

214

1. "Wherewithal shall a young man cleanse his way? by taking heed thereto according to thy word." (Psalms 119:9)
2. "For ever, O Lord, thy word is settled in heaven." (119:89)
3. "Thy word is a lamp unto my feet, and a light unto my path." (119:105)
4. "Heaven and earth shall pass away, but my words shall not pass away." (Matthew 24:35)
5. "O how love I thy law! it is my meditation all the day." (Psalm 119:97)
6. "Great peace have they which love thy law: and nothing shall offend them." (Psalm 119:165)

III. **CONCLUSION**: **"Teach me to do thy will; for thou art my God: thy spirit is good; lead me into the land of uprightness." (Psalms 143:10)**

Section: II

A brief review of: four, 'Personal Life' books, written by: Aimee Filan Anderson and Albert E. Anderson.

A brief review of: four, 'True' Historical Expose¢ books, written by: Albert and Aimee Anderson.

A brief review of our movie, 'A MURDER OF INNOCENCE, written and produced by Shawn Justice and Aimee Filan Anderson.

PERSONAL LIFE SERIES

"BROKEN, YET TRIUMPHANT"
Author: Aimee Filan Anderson

"SUNSHINE THROUGH CLOUDS"
Author: Aimee Filan Anderson
Co-Author: Albert E. Anderson

"OUR AWESOME JOURNEY"
Authors: Albert & Aimee Anderson

"A LEGACY OF LOVE LETTERS"
Author: Aimee Filan Anderson

"I HAVE KEPT THE FAITH"
Authors: Albert & Aimee Anderson

BROKEN, YET TRIUMPHANT -- (1)

BROKEN, YET TRIUMPHANT reveals in fictional form the drama of family suspense in finding the brutally slain bodies of two dear friends (double-murder mystery). It incorporates private episodes that touch the heartstrings, including near death experiences, stolen property, and the fish-bowl existence of the Minister's home through the transparent heart of a Minister's wife.

BROKEN, YET TRIUMPHANT, is a personal story of two people and their family as they walk together in the service of their Master -- their conflicts and their strife -- their tears and their heartaches -- their joys and their victories, but always going onward and upward in their walk with the Lord. You will see their battles, their defeats, and their victories. Often what looks like defeat will be seen later to have been a positive victory. Deliverance was achieved from seemingly insurmountable odds.

No one is an island to himself. Each one touches another. We help or hinder; bless or curse. A blazed trail offers assurance and encouragement. *BROKEN, YET TRIUMPHANT* is written to bless and help other pilgrims on their way to conformity and greater fruitfulness.

Critically acclaimed by churchmen and editors as a dramatic account -- glowing, revealing, and inspiring -- this is a true story

Frank N. McAllister (former superintendent), states in the Preface, "Thank God...as He made a way for the Andersons, He will make a way for you."

SUNSHINE THROUGH CLOUDS –- (2)

Sequel to *BROKEN, YET TRIUMPHANT -- SUNSHINE THROUGH CLOUDS* reveals the continued drama and *agitation* of broken family relationships. This is a sequel to Aimee's first book (1983 & 2001) *BROKEN, YET TRIUMPHANT,* which book reveals the drama of family turmoil, a double-murder mystery, stolen property, near death experiences, and the fish-bowl existence of the Minister's home through the transparent heart of a Minister's wife. Displays in vivid detail the fall-out of broken family relationships and subsequent emotional heartaches.

The last chapter of Aimee's former book, *BROKEN, YET TRIUMPHANT,* contains a courtroom scene. The sequel, *SUNSHINE THROUGH CLOUDS,* under different circumstances, begins in like manner.

This book reveals the passion for fairness and justice, especially in personal or family relationships. It expresses the longing for just and fair judgment to be rendered, with nothing cleverly and deceitfully covered. Failures here will occur in the finite human realm. However, there is a time and place when absolute justice will be meted out. Justice bestowed then will be due to the *qualifications of the Judge.*

SUNSHINE THROUGH CLOUDS demonstrates the life-giving path to take when receiving injustice. Unjust treatment wrongly processed within our spirit only compounds the original problem. This book is sent to those in the eye of the storm. Fix your gaze upon the *Son* and the shadows will disappear. The *sun* is always shining back of the clouds!

OUR AWESOME JOURNEY -- (3)

He was there all the time in our awesome miraculous journey of Faith.

"Words do not seem adequate to describe my parents, Albert and Aimee Anderson. You will love reading about my Dad and Mom's memories. I am so glad that Dad started writing before he became bedridden. You will be blessed beyond words as you read this book." (Debbie Chase)

It is a mystery how God molds and shapes two different lives: preparing them for the beautiful marriage relationship that was originally ordained by God, himself. When these two lives meet, get acquainted, marry each other in Holy matrimony, and become one in the Lord, it truly is awesome and wonderful. It is very inspiring to others when they continue to daily honor the Lord; love each other as husband and wife, as Christ loves the church, and, by loving example, teaching their children to honor the Lord as well. "Them that honor me, I will honor."

Albert Anderson and Aimee Filan were a perfect match, made and developed for each other by the *perfect match maker, God in heaven.*

A LEGACY OF LOVE LETTERS -- (4)

I have always counted it a great privilege that I was born into an awesome Christian family - the oldest child of Albert Emmanuel Anderson and Aimee Donalda Filan Anderson. Because of that great privilege came great responsibilities to which I seemed to run to them with open arms. You see, my parents set such a great example of love, born out of their deep and abiding faith and love for Jesus who was and always has been their source of strength in everything they ever did. Jesus was not someone they called on just when they needed something; he was their everything during the good times as well as the bad. Was their LIFE perfect? By no means! Was their MARRIAGE perfect? Basically, it was! How can I say that? Because Jesus was the center of their marriage and their whole life, and when Jesus has that much control and leadership - then perfection does exist! Even though this book is love letters that were written in the first months of their courtship, engagement, and a few love letters from the first years of their marriage when dad was away on evangelistic meetings, they could have been written 20 - 30 - 40 - or 50 plus years into their relationship - because how they viewed each other and their deep love for each other never wavered or changed! They did not have IPhones, or IPads, or computers, or social media - their communication was verbally, and on paper! I have always admired their love for Jesus and their love for each other, their walk with Jesus, their commitment to each other, their commitment to their 6 children, their commitment to the church even though the church was not always there for them, and their commitment and strong conviction to lead many souls to Jesus over a 60-year span of service to HIM!

I strive to be more like my parents - but more importantly more like Jesus - because that is what matters most. I am proud that my 5 siblings all love Jesus, I am proud that I was raised in a Christian home. I am thankful and proud of the fact I was chosen to be raised by Albert and Aimee! I have carried many responsibilities over the years as a badge of honor because in doing so I did my best to represent Jesus and represent my parents by living the way they wanted me to and trained me to live! Jesus is everything and without HIM, this fantastic, abiding, LOVE would NOT have existed.

I miss you dad! Thank you for your leadership and example of what true love means; I have the assurance I WILL see you again someday in Heaven. Thank you mom for your love, leadership, and example! I appreciate you more than words can say. You are an inspiration to me and to everyone you come in contact with. Never give up! I know you miss dad deeply, but someday you will be reunited with your one true love! Then all of Heaven will rejoice.

Whoever reads this book will be inspired. Treasure your spouse, watch the words that come out of your mouth, live a life devoted to Jesus and it WILL reflect in your love for each other!

With all my love,
Deborah Dawn Anderson Chase

I HAVE KEPT THE FAITH – (5)

As the oldest of the six children of Albert E and Aimee D Anderson, I have always seemed to carry the torch for our family legacy. I have "great" and "awesome" memories of the many sermons my dad preached throughout his years of ministry in the pulpit, as well as the "many" sermons that were preached to us kids before and during our times of discipline after doing something we were told not to do! Both were invaluable in my upbringing; and I will always be grateful for that.

I know beyond a shadow of a doubt that this book will be an invaluable tool for the "new" Christian just beginning his journey, the "seasoned" Christian wanting a deeper walk with the Lord, or the person that is simply "searching" for something that is missing in their lives! Jesus wants to be sought after by all humanity; and it is only after finding "HIM" the giver of life, that true happiness lies. May you be as blessed reading this book as I was living it day in and day out!

(By: Deborah Dawn Anderson Chase)

MOVIE

A MURDER OF INNOCENCE
Based on Aimee Filan Anderson's book,
BROKEN, YET TRIUMPHANT
Co-Producers:
Shawn Justice & Aimee Filan Anderson

The feature-length drama film, A MURDER OF INNOCENCE, follows Aimee, her Pastor husband, Albert, and their six children: Debbie, Becky, Mary, Eunice, Mark, and Jonathan, as they discover through terrible tragedy, that: "Faith in the night as well as the day," "Praying without Ceasing," and, "Praising the Lord, throughout the Day and Night," brings the "Wonderful Peace of God," that floods our hearts and lives.

A MURDER OF INNOCENCE, is based on the life and family of, Albert and Aimee Anderson. AMOI is a female driven, emotionally charged feature film that explores faith, fear, and God's sovereignty, This, award-winning drama is based on the true-life story of Aimee Filan Anderson, who's powerful tale comes to life on the big screen.

The movie follows Aimee, her Pastor husband Albert, and their six children; Debbie, Becky, Mary, Eunice, Mark and Jonathan as they move to Sequim, Washington. Shortly after establishing themselves the Anderson's grew close to an older couple who are very active in the church. After Aimee's strange premonitions the Anderson's discover the bodies of their murdered friends.

With a killer at large, and little evidence for leads, fear and suspicion run rampant in the small town. The Andersons encountered the victims of the tragedy that shocked and paralyzed the small town and the ensuing trial, lasted five (5) days.

The local sheriff attempts to keep the peace, but finds it challenging. For Aimee, a very real fear takes hold that takes a supernatural faith to overcome.

Because of God's AMAZING LOVE, freely given to us, through all of the many years, our beautiful and sweet, *YOUTHFUL, AMAZING LOVE* for each other, remained true and faithful during all of the trials and tribulations that came to test our love for God and for each other and our children's love for Jesus Christ our Lord and Saviour! As long as we are in this World, with God's grace and help, we can face and overcome the trials and tribulations that are hurled at us, in the Wonderful Name of, Jesus Christ, our precious Saviour! Praise God!

Righteousness is true Justice and True Justice is always fair – otherwise there is no Justice. Without Justice, there is no Freedom. When there is no Freedom, anarchy reigns

Albert and Aimee Anderson heard cries of the wounded (as true Shepherds do) in two different church denominations and personally became involved in mending wounds. In so doing they found that the price was extremely high and became wounded themselves.

Yes, their David and Goliath struggle against denominational powers (unscrupulous and unethical conduct by church officials) has taken its toll. They could have been "bought off" and chosen comfort instead of sacrifice and commitment to Scripture, but for them righteousness forbids it.

Failure to obey God's Word in areas of honesty, integrity, and moral uprightness, reaps a terrible whirlwind of sorrow and regret.

Promoting the guilty while punishing the innocent shall not receive Divine blessing.

God's laws and God's dealings with humanity are based on absolute Justice. Our God is not partial nor does He have 'favorites' whom he allows to get by with sins for which He condemns others. The Apostle Paul declared to all those in attendance at the household of Cornelius, "Of a truth I perceive that God is no respecter of persons: (Acts 10:34)

When Albert's Pastoral Ministry was stolen from him, as a result of 'whistle-blowing' on the Church Hierarchy's corruption, we felt led to do as the Bible says when they won't listen to you – *write it down.* Thus, the four books, *WHITED SEPULCHRES, A GENERATION OF VIPERS, WHITE COLLAR CRIME IN THE CHURCH,* and *GRAND JURY MYSTERY,* were written and published. After my husband died in 2013, I just wanted to forget those four expose' books and that very painful period in my life, when my dear precious husband was so unjustly excommunicated from two different major church denominations for exposing the 'Church Leadership Corruption'.

My husband and I, at different times, entertained in our home U.S. Federal Agents, who gathered copies of legal documents and other information; – two Criminal IRS Agents, and one FBI Agent, and two U.S. Criminal Attorneys from the Federal Justice Department in Washington D.C. This, Grand Jury Mystery, along with the evil excommunication story, is all documented in our four Expose' true-story books: – *WHITED SEPULCHRES, GENERATION OF VIPERS, WHITE COLLAR CRIME IN THE CHURCH, and GRAND JURY MYSTERY.* A brief description of each of those four books follows:

CHURCH INVESTIGATION SERIES

"WHITED SEPULCHRES"
"A GENERATION OF VIPERS"
"WHITE COLLAR CRIME IN THE CHURCH"
"GRAND JURY MYSTERY"

The
ELITE MAFIA RULES:
MUZZLE THE MESSENGERS
AT ANY COST

* * * * *

The most powerful, exclusive, dominating
group – a law unto themselves

* * * * *

BUT THE MESSENGERS
REFUSED TO BE SILENCED

WHITED SEPULCHRES -- (1)

This book is more than an expose' of one scandal, in one denomination, in part of the country. It is autopsy on the politically correct, politically powerful and politically motivated church of today.

Spiritual devastation resulting from unfaithful or flawed leadership will be poignantly declared. Truth must not be altered, watered down, or compromised.

Church leaders and parishioners hold the United States government and world leaders "accountable" for their actions. Likewise, the U.S. government and people of the world also have a right to hold church leaders and parishioners "accountable" for their actions, as well.

It is spiritual high treason for church leaders to use the "CHURCH" as a safe sanctuary from civil prosecution when committing ungodly and illegal acts. The Head of the church, Jesus Christ, with scathing denunciation rebuked the Pharisees of His day for their spiritual hypocrisy. For they self-righteously defended their own sins against God while they were quick to condemn those unable to defend themselves. God has one standard for both the church and the world. *"God is no respecter of persons."*

For the time is come that judgment must begin at the house of God: and if it first begin at us, what shall the end be of them that obey not the gospel of God. And if the righteous scarcely be saved, where shall the ungodly and sinner appear? (I Peter 4:17-18; Ezekiel 9:6)

Without question, any level of Christian leadership is an awesome responsibility. Failure here produces waves of destructive influence that cannot be measured. The "called" ministry, whether pastoral or strictly executive and administrative, deals in the currency of eternal souls. Thus, a spiritual, yet practical, idealism must guide all leaders in their sphere of ministry. The apostle Paul states this succinctly in II Corinthians 6:3 when he says: "Giving no offense in anything that the ministry be not blamed."

A GENERATION OF VIPERS -- (2)

This is an exposé dealing with corruption within evangelical church leadership and consequent effects therefrom. It is the story of the unscrupulous and unethical conduct by officials of two large evangelical organizations. Spiritual devastation resulting from unfaithful or flawed leadership will be poignantly declared. Truth must not be altered, watered down, or compromised. Accepting the truth of real-life experience can be painful to hear about and very difficult to resolve.

Vigilant corrections on the road of life are essential if we would arrive at the intended goal. When our astronauts fired their rockets to blast out of earth's gravitational pull and aimed for the moon, constant computerized navigational corrections were made to enable their orbiting the moon upon arrival. When leaving the earth, an ever so slight degree of error, would have ultimately placed the astronauts far from the gravitational pull of the moon and their desired orbit.

Laws, rules (including United States Constitution), and bylaws, are not evil in themselves; they only become evil when church and/ or civil leadership use them for evil intent or purposes, rather than for the good of all people.

If the Pastors of this nation do not do what God has called them to do, this nation is a ship without a rudder, nor a radar. This book is about the disaster that happens when Pastors are derelict in their duty.

Daily we hear about sin, heartaches, sorrow, and pain. Instead, we would rather be encouraged, hear a note of victory, and have our spirits lifted. And, certainly a joyful word is often needed. Yet, distasteful medicine may prolong life, if not provide a cure. There is a time and place for self-examination. The apostle Paul exhorted, "Examine yourselves, whether ye be in the faith; prove your own selves." (II Corinthians 13:5a)

Many individuals may not want to take spiritual inventory because they fear the truth. But it is far better to discover the true state of spiritual life now when remedy is possible than to sleep peacefully on and die in sin. The Bible says, "Examine Yourselves, whether ye be in the Faith;"

WHITE COLLAR CRIME IN THE CHURCH – (3)

WHITE COLLAR CRIME IN THE CHURCH is an expose' of the ongoing miscarriage of justice and intrigue, even in the clergy. The conspiracy deepens. Others are snared into the wicked scheme of events: U.S. Justice Department, FBI, Criminal Division of the IRS, and others.

A portrait of where American Christianity has declined is displayed in the skulduggery of some Clergy who have become inveterate Hypocrites. Bullies in the Pulpit, who are trying to take over the churches of today. If possible, these Bullies who are controlled by their thirst of power and greed will rule and reign with cruel threats. They intimidate, manipulate, and coerce their followers (Bully Buddies) in order to gain absolute control.

It is apparent that people in the church with power, might, and money can be criminals and escape punishment. Maybe politics has played a role after all. Innocent people continue to suffer as victims of the heavy-handed unscrupulous techniques of the Bullies and their Bully Buddies.

District and National church officials became insidious in their hypocrisy. Church leaders who have become Bullies and Bully Buddies, a dominating and exclusive group of people, now are the Church Mafia? They subjugate and tyrannize their subordinates.

Compromise and conflict of interest surrounding this ongoing saga has grown. In addition to the involvement of District and National Church Officials, it now includes U.S. Government Officials who have been snared into the wicked scheme of events.

America is like a sinking ship that needs to dial Heaven's 911 and cry out in repentance to God Almighty for forgiveness and help. In order for the Church and our Nation to be restored, some church officials/leaders need to repent and make restitution to those whom they have so sinfully injured.

GRAND JURY MYSTERY -- (4)

GRAND JURY MYSTERY is an expose' of ongoing miscarriage of justice and intrigue, even in the clergy. It is apparent that people in the church with power, might, and money can also be criminals and escape punishment. Maybe politics has played a role after all. You be the judge. Innocent people become victims and continue to suffer under the heavy-handed unscrupulous techniques of Bullies and their Bully Buddies. Church mafia! Imposters!

Righteousness is true Justice and True Justice is always fair – otherwise there is no Justice. Without Justice, there is no Freedom. When there is no freedom, anarchy reigns. As responsible *United States citizens,* let us contend for our *American* heritage before we lose it completely – *"One Nation under <u>GOD</u>, Indivisible, with Liberty and Justice for all."*

The conflict of interest issue is rampant in both the church government and the legal justice system of this world. As a result, many times fairness and equality are cast aside and disregarded as unimportant. The saga of sinful scheming and conspiracy continued for years and the cover-up of the corruption continues to unravel, as the curtain is slowly opened, unveiling some of the mysterious cover-up.

GRAND JURY MYSTERY is the mysterious ongoing miscarriage of justice and intrigue in the church leadership and the legal justice system of this world. It reveals how those who question established authority can be trampled on, crushed, thrown aside, and shunned while at the same time *"Moral Values"* are all mixed up and of no value.

The great mysterious secrecy surrounding the *"QUESTIONABLE"* grand jury investigation helped hide the U.S. attorney conflict of interest. The American grand jury system can be good but we have discovered that it also can be very dangerous to justice because of all the secrecy; which enables potential miscarriage of justice at the highest levels of government. At all levels of the Church and U.S. Government there has been cover-up and more cover-up of the cover-up. The Grand Jury secrecy/mystery has greatly helped to conceal the corruption, and the corrupt cover-up of the corruption. For years, the U.S. Federal agents and the District and National Church Officials carried on with their *big ruse.*

The sad truth is, those in leadership often fall prey to the lust for power and control. Church officials rely on subterfuge to conceal their unholy deeds. People with power, might, and money can be criminals and escape punishment. FBI updates, Sheriff Detective report, U.S. Justice Department personnel in Seattle, Washington, and Washington D.C., a marriage certificate / license, and personal testimony confirm the truth about this very mysterious grand jury criminal investigation. Some of this unbelievable, yet authentic, information we now share with you in this documentary / expose, the fourth of a series.

GRAND JURY MYSTERY continues to expose the corruption and cover-up of the same in some of the highest reaches of the Church and U.S. government. Both civil and criminal investigations were botched (as well as the original "conflict of interest" investigation by dishonest church officials) which compounded the evil of the original Care-Net Outreach fraud. How the Church and Federal cases were handled is closely related. As a result of these unjust actions there is no justice and no closure, even though grand jury secrets are now being exposed.

"As many as I love, I rebuke and chasten: be zealous therefore, and repent.

Behold, I stand at the door, and knock: if any man hear my voice, and open the door, I will come in to him, and will sup with him, and he with me.

To him that overcometh will I grant to sit with me in my throne, even as I also overcame, and am set down with my father in his throne.

He that hath an ear, let him hear what the Spirit saith unto the churches:" (Revelation 3:19-22)

PEACE

Radio message preached by Albert
In Walla Walla, Washington
November 15, 1953,

Just this past Tuesday, we celebrated the signing of the Armistice which was the official declaration of peace at the close of World War I. Yet there has been no lasting peace. Why? It would not be wrong to come to the conclusion that the reason lies in the fact that some have not lived by the principles of that peace treaty. And the Bible tells us there will be no lasting peace as long as men reject the "Prince of Peace," Jesus Christ.

Over 1900 years ago an infinitely greater peace treaty was provided for "whosoever will" would meet its conditions – that is, the sacrifice of the Lord Jesus Christ for the sins of the world. In a certain sense, these two treaties are alike in that peace is in effect only as those concerned apprehend and "live by" the principles of the treaty. And it follows that the reason the lesser peace treaty, concerning war, has proved ineffective is because men have not lived by the principles of the greater peace treaty – "salvation through Christ." And as long as men refuse and reject the "Prince of Peace" Jesus Christ, as the Lord of their lives, just so long will the world be in turmoil and unrest. There can be no real peace until men allow the principles of Christ to rule and guide their lives. When multitudes refuse to acknowledge the claims of Christ, of necessity world conditions will be in a condition of strife and war. What is the world – wide condition of strife and hate; but an evident token of the unrest and strife in the <u>individual</u> human heart. Collective unrest is but an indication of unrest in the individual.

From the time of the annunciation of the birth of Christ by the angels to His death, peace of spirit, soul, and body was the will and plan of God.

The apostle Paul in writing to the Romans in the fifteenth chapter and 33rd verse says, "Now the God of peace be with you all." Think of it! The God of PEACE, the one who desires to implant peace and security in the human heart. And in Ephesians 2:14 it says: "For He is our peace," So to the person who is willing to come to the lowly Christ, then to that person shall be ministered the "peace of God."

Oh so many people today are fidgety and uneasy; not able to relax for a moment – often the reason being they're afraid to stop and think of where they are headed. And do not think for a moment that I will pray for you to have rest in your soul apart from an absolute surrender to the Lord Jesus Christ. If more unrest in your soul would drive some of you to Christ Jesus then may the mercy of God send unrest and discomfort into your heart until you'll cry out to God to have mercy on your poor sinful soul. There is no rest outside of a personal knowledge of Christ as your Saviour and Lord.

In I Corinthians 14:33 the scripture tells us that God is the author of peace. Now if He is the author of peace then He is the one to go to in order to secure peace of heart. Then, God, being the "author" of peace; who is the author of unrest and anguish of Soul? Since it does not come from God, there can be only one other source that is, Satan and sin. The Bible again tells us in Isaiah 57:20-21, "But the wicked are like the troubled sea, when it cannot rest, whose waters cast up mire and dirt. There is no peace, saith my God, to the wicked." The Bible is very plain and explicit isn't it? You who are without Christ as your personal Saviour just simply cannot have peace in your hearts. Unrest and a condition of turmoil in human hearts is nothing other than the work of the adversary of our souls and the results of sin.

Those listening to me this afternoon without Christ as your Saviour will never have peace until you surrender your life to the one who died for your sins. You may seek to busy yourself more in your business, your family, your home, or perhaps in pleasure and worldly amusements; but not a single one of those things will suffice to bring the Peace of God into your souls. The Bible says in Romans 5:1, "Therefore being justified by faith, we have peace with God through our Lord Jesus Christ." So you see true peace which comes from God is ministered unto you through no other avenue than by and through the Son of God, Jesus Christ:

Jesus said unto His disciples, "Peace I leave with you, my peace I give unto you: not as the world giveth, give I unto you. Let not your heart be troubled, neither let it be afraid." (John 14:27) And again in John 16:33, "These things I have spoken unto you, that in me ye might have peace. In the world you shall have tribulation: but be of good cheer; I have overcome the world."

No one could help but agree that the will and desire of God for all mankind is that they shall have peace in their hearts and be at peace with their God. And the only reason this isn't accomplished is because men and women simply do not come to Him and allow Him to give them peace. Perhaps the reason lies deeper than what it appears on the surface. Oh, yes, many would like to have their fears taken away and know a real peace in their souls; but too many want to go on living just the way they are and still experience the blessing of the peace of God in their lives. In other words, they want the blessing, peace, without having anything to do with the blesser, Christ. And yet without the one who gives the blessing of peace in your heart, can you ever know real and lasting peace. What does Isaiah say again, "Your sins have separated you from your God." Why are people in America and across the world in unrest? Simply, because, of their sins.

Get right with God and then you will have every right to ask God for peace in your heart; but more than likely, you won't even have to ask once you have been justified by the blood of Christ.

Politicians are saying, Peace, Peace, trying somehow to gain world peace. And, yet, the Bible says when they cry such a thing, sudden destruction cometh upon them. Why? Simply, because they have failed to live by the principles of the Prince of Peace, Jesus Christ. My friend, before you pray for World peace, you ought to repent of your own sins and get right with God, and then you can rightly pray for world peace. What do you want world peace for? So you can go on living in your sins without fear of harm or danger? Is it not true that many people want peace in the world so that they can go on in their business without being molested, in other words thinking only of the present without ever a thought for their eternal, never – dying soul? It's time millions forgot about world peace until they first made their peace with God. It's time America turns back to God and then she can rightly believe God to spare her sons and daughters. But, I fear my friends, if millions of American citizens do not get right with God, we cannot believe Him for protection upon us and of peace in the world. Peace of heart in the individual through Jesus Christ will bring peace on a National and International scale.

I close this book with another one of Albert's Gospel Messages that tell the story of how we, Albert and I, endeavored to live our lives.

Praise the Lord!

BITTER or BETTER

Scripture: "Let all bitterness, and wrath, and anger, and clamour, and evil speaking, be put away from you, with all malice: And be ye kind one to another, tenderhearted, forgiving one another, even as God for Christ's sake hath forgiven you." (Ephesians 4:31, 32)

INTRODUCTION: Sooner or later BAD things---hurts, disappointments, wrongs done to us happen to everyone. No one is immune. To suffer because of our own foolishness, because we made a bad decision, because of our own sin, in one sense is to be expected; but to suffer because of someone else's wrongdoing is quite another. However, we need to remember, when we suffer because of another's sin, we still are free to make a personal decision. Will I become BITTER or will I choose to become BETTER? No one else can make that decision for us, we must do it ourselves. Consider real people in God's Word who had to make this decision.

III. JOSEPH:

    A. Genesis 37 — 50

        1. Hated by his older brothers.
        2. Sold into slavery by those same brothers.
        3. Potiphar's wife endeavored to seduce him; because of his staying true to God and being lied about by Potiphar's wife, he was thrown into prison.
        4. In prison, he became a faithful slave / servant.

5. Joseph simply kept on serving God where he was and all without BITTERNESS.

6. His faithfulness to God—without the bondage of bitterness, caused him to be elevated in responsibility and ultimately became the means of saving his own family from starvation. In short, he became a BETTER person!

II. THE APOSTLE PAUL:

A. "Are they ministers of Christ? (I speak as a fool) I am more; in labours more abundant, in stripes above measure, in prisons more frequent, in deaths oft. Of the Jews five times received I forty stripes save one. Thrice was I beaten with rods, once was I stoned, thrice I suffered shipwreck, a night and a day I have been in the deep; In journeyings often, in perils of waters, in perils of robbers, in perils by mine own countrymen, in perils by the heathen, in perils in the city, in perils in the wilderness, in perils in the sea, in perils among false brethren, In weariness and painfulness, in watchings often, in hunger and thirst, in fastings often, in cold and nakedness. Beside those things that are without, that which cometh upon me daily, the care of all the churches." (II Corinthians 11:23-28)

1. Yet in spite of all these hardships, Paul kept a sweet spirit and wrote a major part of the New Testament.
2. You will find no trace of BITTERNESS in the attitude and spirit of the Apostle Paul.
3. He became BETTER.
4. "For I determined not to know anything among you, save Jesus Christ, and him crucified." (I Corinthians 2:2)

III. JOHN, THE BELOVED:

    A. Exiled on the Isle of Patmos for the testimony of Jesus Christ.

        1. Though separated from family and friends, God gave him visions and revelations concerning end-time events---things which will be fulfilled perhaps in our lifetime.
        2. You will find no BITTERNESS in the attitude and spirit of John---only a willingness to be used of God. Thus, he became BETTER!

IV. CONCLUSION: No one can control all the circumstances and events that come to us day by day. Oftentimes things happen which we have no control over. However, each one of us CAN control our REACTION to what transpires in our lives. We can make a conscious choice whether we will allow the events of our lives to make us BITTER or BETTER. We can become BITTER as acid---mean, sour, miserable to be with or near---or we can use (with God's grace and help) the happenings of our lives to make us more loving, kind, considerate of others---more like Jesus! Consider Jesus: "He is despised and rejected of men; a man of sorrows, and acquainted with grief: and we hid as it were our faces from him; he was despised, and we esteemed him not. Surely he hath borne our griefs, and carried our sorrows: yet we did esteem him stricken, smitten of God, and afflicted. But he was wounded for our transgressions, he was bruised for our iniquities: the chastisement of our peace was upon him; and with his stripes we are healed. All we like sheep have gone astray; we have turned everyone to his own way; and the Lord hath laid upon him the iniquity of us all." (Isaiah 53:3-6)

"Hast thou not known? Hast thou not heard, that the everlasting God, the Lord, the Creator of the ends of the earth, fainteth not, neither is weary? there is no searching of his understanding.

He giveth power to the faint; and to them that have no might he increaseth strength.

Even the youths shall faint and be weary, and the young men shall utterly fall:

But they that wait upon the Lord shall renew their strength; they shall mount up with wings as eagles; they shall run, and not be weary; and they shall walk, and not faint." (Isaiah 40:28–31)

About The Authors

Aimee Filan Anderson, daughter of Olaus and Minnie Filan, was born near Hay, Washington, in Whitman County and grew up on a wheat ranch. After high school graduation from Wa Hi in Walla Walla, Washington, she attended Northwest College in Kirkland, Washington.

Albert Emmanuel Anderson, son of Albert and Hazel Anderson, was born near Crocker, South Dakota, in Clark County and graduated from Clark High School. In 1952, he graduated with a B.A. degree in Bible from Central Bible College in Springfield, Missouri. After graduation, he began evangelistic ministry.

Albert married Aimee Filan, April 9, 1954, in Walla Walla, Washington. While on their honeymoon, he was ordained as an Assemblies of God (A/G) minister in his home church at Clark, South Dakota.

With his wife, Aimee, they traveled together for almost three years, holding evangelistic meetings until taking their first church in February 1957 – shortly after their first child Deborah Dawn was born.

Sectional District offices Albert has held: include Sunday School Representative, Youth Director, Camp Speaker, and Presbyter. On June 19, 1994, he resigned as pastor of the Ellensburg First Assembly of God, after a ten-year pastorate there.

On April 9, 1954, Aimee married Albert E. Anderson, an evangelist and minister in the Assemblies of God. Together they traveled throughout the U.S. while holding evangelistic meetings, until they accepted their first pastorate in 1957.

For fifty-nine years, lacking one month to the day (as of March 9, 2013), Aimee was a minister's wife. She has ministered as a Sunday School Superintendent, church pianist, and a leader in church organizations. She, also, still is an Ordained (THE FELLOWSHIP) Minister. Over the past years, Aimee helped her husband pastor ten (10) different churches throughout the State of Washington. While their six children, Deborah, Rebecca, Mary, Eunice, Mark, and Jonathan were still living at home, the Anderson family performed numerous musical concerts.

In addition to being blessed with four daughters and two sons, their family now includes four sons-in-law, one daughter-in-law, thirty-four (34) grandchildren (including the ones who have married into our family), and twenty-seven (27) great grandchildren which brings the grand total to seventy-two (72) children, grandchildren and great grandchildren. All are precious gifts of God sent from Heaven for us to raise for His Glory and Honor. Praise the Lord!

April 9, 2013, was Albert and Aimee's 59th anniversary, which they missed celebrating together on this earth, by only one month to the day. All praise be to God for all of those wonderful years of love and companionship!

Aimee has authored and/or co-authored (with her husband, Albert E. Anderson) nine (9) books, including this one, **I HAVE KEPT THE FAITH (2021),** and she has co-produced one (1) movie, **A MURDER OF INNOCENCE (2018).**

Aimee authored her first book *BROKEN, YET TRIUMPHANT,* in **1983**. It is a, *Memoir,* based upon her true-life story. The minister husband, Albert, and his wife, Aimee, make a terrible and heart-breaking discovery when they find the bodies of their dear friends, who had been violently murdered. They chose to deal with these untimely deaths, double-murder mystery, and terrorizing fear, other near-death experiences, and trials of faith, by utilizing their strong faith in the Lord.

SUNSHINE THROUGH CLOUDS, in **2001**, is the sequel to

her first book, and her deceased husband became the co-author. A courtroom, and familial drama – the way of justice and forgiveness is not always an easy path followed.

Albert and Aimee, then co-authored a series of books (4), on the corruption that is often present within the Church Leadership and United States Government. It is nothing but the candid truth of illegal activities that occurred in churches from the very people who often preach about following God's laws. The Corruption revealed in the Church leadership, years ago, is still prevalent, today, 2021, in the Church leadership and United States Government, Political World.

The first of the Expose' Book Series was, *WHITED SEPULCHRES,* in **1996**, followed by its sequel, *A GENERATION OF VIPERS,* in **2001**. Thereafter, they co-authored its sequel, *WHITE COLLAR CRIME IN THE CHURCH,* in **2004**, and its sequel, *GRAND JURY MYSTERY,* in **2008**.

Aimee and Albert co-authored their fascinating love story, action-filled story-book (their MEMOIR), based on some of their true-life experiences. Aimee finished and published, *OUR AWESOME JOURNEY,* in **2014**. after her dear husband, Albert, was called to his Heavenly home. Aimee, then authored, *A LEGACY OF LOVE LETTERS,* in **2019**, Followed by this book, *I HAVE KEPT THE FAITH,* in **2021**.

The movie, *A MURDER OF INNOCENCE* (Trailer and personal Interview with Aimee and her four daughters, Debbie, Becky, Mary, and Eunice), was produced in **(2018),** based on Aimee's first book, *BROKEN, YET TRIUMPHANT.*

Even on his 'death bed,'
During his dying days,
Albert Emmanuel Anderson
Continued to preach and/or teach, and live the
Word of God!

"I, (Albert) have fought a good fight, I have finished my course, I have kept the faith:"

"Henceforth there is laid up for me a crown of righteousness, which the Lord, the righteous judge, shall give me at that day: and not to me only, but unto all them also that love his appearing." (II Timothy 4:7-8)

Albert Emmanuel Anderson,
remained Faithful to the Lord,
And to his wife, and family:
To the very end of his life on this earth!

PRAISE THE LORD!

God gave Albert and Aimee grace and strength to endure the *test of faith!* Praise the Lord! God enabled them to *'love their enemies'* and keep their hearts full of love for the wounded and bleeding. They still loved the Lord; God means everything to them. They, both, made a 'choice' to become **'Better'** instead of 'Bitter' no matter what the 'Trial' and 'Test of their Faith' that they had to endure and go through. We give all glory and honor to our, Wonderful Lord Jesus Christ, and Saviour, God Almighty! "Praise the Lord."

After Albert was taken to his Heavenly Home, Aimee and her family still need to daily look to the Lord for grace and strength to endure the trials and tests of faith that God allows to come their way.

"No weapon that is formed against thee shall prosper; and every tongue that shall rise against thee in judgment thou shalt condemn. This is the heritage of the servants of the Lord, and their righteousness is of me, saith the Lord." (Isaiah 54:17)

"If my people, which are called by my name, shall humble themselves, and pray, and seek my face, and turn from their wicked ways; then will I hear from heaven, and will forgive their sin, and will heal their land." (II Chronicles 7:14)

"The Lord is my light and my salvation; whom shall I fear? The Lord is the strength of my life; of whom shall I be afraid?" (Psalm 27:1)

"And then shall many be offended, and shall betray one another, and shall hate one another.

And many false prophets shall rise, and shall deceive many.

And because iniquity shall abound, the love of many shall wax cold.

But he that shall endure unto the end, the same shall be saved." (Matthew 24:10-13)

"This is the day which the Lord hath made;
we will rejoice and be glad in it." (Psalms 118:24)

"I will bless the Lord at all times:
His praise shall continually be in my mouth."
(Psalms 34:1)

"My Heavenly Father, I love you,
and,
I thank you for your Wonderful Love
given to me and my family all of these many years!"

"PRAISE THE LORD!

Printed in the United States
by Baker & Taylor Publisher Services